SHAMANISM
FOR
EVERY DAY

SHAMANISM
FOR
EVERY DAY

365 Journeys

Mara Bishop

CITADEL PRESS
Kensington Publishing Corp.
www.kensingtonbooks.com

CITADEL PRESS BOOKS are published by
Kensington Publishing Corp.
119 West 40th Street
New York, NY 10018

All Kensington titles, imprints, and distributed lines are available at special quantity discounts for bulk purchases for sales promotions, premiums, fund-raising, educational, or institutional use. Special book excerpts or customized printings can also be created to fit specific needs. For details, write or phone the office of the Kensington sales manager: Kensington Publishing Corp., 119 West 40th Street, New York, NY 10018, attn: Sales Department; phone 1-800-221-2647.

CITADEL PRESS and the Citadel logo are Reg. U.S. Pat. & TM Off.

ISBN-13: 978-0-8065-4106-8
ISBN-10: 0-8065-4106-7

First Citadel trade paperback printing: April 2021

10 9 8 7 6 5 4 3 2 1

Printed in the United States of America

Electronic edition:

ISBN-13: 978-0-8065-4107-5 (e-book)
ISBN-10: 0-8065-4107-5 (e-book)

For V

Contents

Introduction—Coming Home • 1

Why I Created Shamanism
for Every Day: 365 Journeys • 4

How to Use Shamanism
for Every Day: 365 Journeys • 6

What Is Shamanism? • 9

How to Journey • 14

Daily Journeys • 39

1 *Beginning*

2 *Direct Revelation*

3 *Power Animal*

4 *Drumming*

5 *"Seeing" Like a Shaman*

6 *Web of Connection*

7 *Balance: Upright
in Upheaval*

8 *Heartstorming*

9 *Spirit Teacher*

10 *Experience Your Body*

11 *The Next Normal*

12 *Underwater*

13 *Signs in Nature*

14 *Air*

15 *Something New*

16 *Invisible and Visible*

17 *Open Guidance*

18 *Vulnerability*

19 *Energy Focus*

20 *Spirit in Everything*

21 *Heaven on Earth*

22 *Answers*

23 *Community*

24 *Directions*

25 *Gifts for the Earth*

26 *Radiant Love*

27 *Inner Wisdom*

28 Responsibility

29 Shadow and Light

30 Inclusivity

31 What Does My
    Body Need?

32 Play

33 Adapting to Time
    and Place

34 Roots and Branches

35 Be Kind, Live Longer

36 Humility

37 Quality Time

38 Honoring Our Tools

39 The Elements Within You

40 Authenticity

41 What Needs Seeing?

42 Power of the Invisible:
    Sparking Change

43 Honoring Elders

44 Pronoia

45 States of Consciousness

46 Creativity and
    Imagination

47 Heartbreak

48 Loving Yourself

49 Rocks

50 The Void

51 Sexuality

52 Mushrooming Networks

53 Lion

54 What's Missing?

55 Wise Power

56 Perfection

57 I Wish or I Am

58 Crow

59 Creativity

60 Religion and Spirituality

61 Metamotivation

62 Conscious Technology

63 Your Garden Sanctuary

64 Thriving in Chaos, Step 1:
    Focused Observation

65 Thriving in Chaos, Step 2:
    Conscious Stillness

66 Thriving in Chaos, Step 3:
    Deliberate Action

67 Clear Sight

68 Animal Love

69 Dream Guidance

70 Art

71 Working with Fire

72 The Power of Rest

73 Environmental
    Supplements

74 East

75 Rain

76 Open Guidance

77 The Science of Silence

78 Managing Change
    and Volatility

79 Becoming Earth

80 Valuing Time
81 The Bee
82 Quick Calm
83 I Have Everything I Need
84 Laughter
85 Animal Spirit Sight
86 Mental Health
87 Feeling Capable
88 Unexpected Kindness
89 Nourishing Foods
90 Love Manifesting Love
91 Initiations
92 Future Self
93 Honoring Your Body
94 Healing Springs
95 Overcoming Fear
96 Strengths
97 In the Wind
98 Service at Home
99 Fairy Magic
100 Awakening Wisdom:
     Ancestors
101 Awakening Wisdom:
     Descendants
102 Unhealthy Habits
103 Healing Stories
104 Natural Rhythms
105 Pause to Rest
106 Grief
107 Space

108 Sensual Enjoyment
109 Thank You
110 Healing Movement
111 Hard to Love
112 Gift of Loneliness
113 Kindness to Wildlife
114 What Needs Hearing?
115 Warming Sun
116 Dreaming a New Dream
117 Building Bridges
118 Boundaries of Forgiveness
119 Moderation
120 Starlight
121 Unwelcome Thoughts
122 Self-Compassion
123 Journeying Through Time
124 Roses
125 Signs in Nature
126 Regret
127 South
128 When Things Fall Apart
129 Healthy Vulnerability
130 Getting It Done
131 Water
132 Point of Birth
133 Human Love
134 Stone
135 Back in Time to Love
     Yourself as a Baby
136 Your Living Space

137 Speak Up, Stay Quiet
138 Play in Nature
139 Flow
140 Bird's-Eye View
141 Violet
142 Grounding
143 Attracting Kindness
144 Rest and Rejuvenation
145 Answers
146 Service at Work
147 Breathe In, Breathe Out
148 Shame and Guilt
149 Faith
150 Pure Joy
151 Freedom
152 Open Guidance
153 Healing Garden
154 Last Day
155 Love in the Present
156 Sacrifice
157 What Needs My
    Attention Today?
158 Money
159 Singing with Spirits
160 Appreciation
161 What's the Rush?
162 Empathic Overload
163 Healthy Compassion
164 Healing with Nature
165 Easing Burdens

166 Party!
167 Feeling Powerful
168 Kindness and Assumptions
169 Your Body
170 Animal Family
171 Next Steps
172 Being Prepared
173 Unconditional Love
174 Giving Gifts
175 Silence
176 Snowy Landscapes
177 Cycles of Rest
178 New Heights
179 West
180 Receiving Gifts
181 Ambiguity
182 Mothers
183 Celebrating Transitions
184 Writing for Healing
185 Overwhelmed
186 Dedication and Discipline
187 Mud Bath
188 What Needs Seeing?
189 This Moment
190 Bones
191 Practicing Kindness
192 Plenty
193 Blessing with Words
194 True Nature
195 Receiving Love

196 Altar

197 Indulgence and Abstinence

198 Being in Service

199 Spirits of the Land

200 Finding Joy in
    Difficult Times

201 Gifts of Interconnection

202 Power Symbol

203 Peace

204 Body Scan: Upper

205 Body Scan: Lower

206 Healing Art

207 Pure Air

208 Restful Sounds

209 Opportunities

210 Night Sky

211 Emotional Health

212 Giving Love

213 Something New

214 Who Needs My Kindness
    Today?

215 Fathers

216 Physical Energy

217 Back in Time to Love
    Yourself as a Child

218 Healing Old Wounds

219 Honoring the Land

220 Reading the Environment

221 Simplifying

222 Power Song

223 Honoring Spirit Teachers

224 What Needs Hearing?

225 New Perspectives

226 Facing Fears

227 Cool Water

228 North

229 Answers

230 The Dynamics of Eating

231 Planet Love

232 What Doesn't Belong?

233 Limiting Beliefs

234 Fire and Ritual

235 Internal Dialogue

236 Blind Spots

237 Lighten Up

238 Rest and Temperature

239 Taking Action

240 Kindness for Yourself

241 Why Me?

242 Appreciation

243 Time Crunch

244 Dropping Form

245 Relationship Help

246 Your Sacred Space

247 Provisions

248 Younger Self

249 See Me

250 Happy Memories

251 Forgiving Someone

252 Receiving Divine Love

253 Larger Lessons

254 Social Service

255 Crystals

256 Healing from Loss

257 Celebration

258 Stagnation

259 Open Guidance

260 Disappointment

261 Power of Words

262 Kindness

263 Strong Energy Boundaries

264 Insect Eyes

265 Intuitive Connection

266 Patience

267 Confidence

268 Turn It Over

269 Passion

270 What Is Not Mine?

271 Removing What Is
    Not Mine

272 Practical Love

273 Your Body

274 Signs and Omens

275 Ancient Land

276 Sky/Above

277 Inner Critic

278 Disintegration

279 Dolphin

280 Another Culture

281 Peace

282 Back in Time to Love
    Yourself as a Teen

283 Emotional Energy

284 Discipline

285 Play with a Helping Spirit

286 Rest from Work

287 Deeper Kindness

288 New Levels

289 Nourishing Relationships

290 Love Balm

291 Vulnerabilities

292 Ceremony for
    Boosting Power

293 What Needs Seeing?

294 Gratitude of the Spirits

295 Tree Power

296 Setting Things Right

297 Clearing Space

298 Dancing

299 Creation

300 Animal Blessings

301 Turning the Tables

302 Foods to Avoid

303 Feeling Supported

304 Honoring Those
    Who Came Before

305 Forgiving Yourself

306 Soothing Care

307 Remembering

308 Clearing Emotions

309 Your Effect on Others

310 Love for the Divine

311 Air and Breath

312 Answers

313 Silence

314 Service in the Community

315 Rest Your Body

316 Overlooked Abundance

317 Truth

318 Appreciation

319 Stop Saying That

320 Singing

321 Earth/Below

322 Time Off

323 Dream Theme

324 Gathering Nuts

325 Ideal Relationships

326 Favorite Place

327 Ancestors

328 Anxiety Antidote

329 Open Heart

330 What Needs Hearing?

331 Water Creatures

332 Belief into Action

333 Next Steps

334 Play Break

335 Ceremony to Honor Someone

336 Visioning

337 Vision into Action

338 Life Goals

339 Perceiving Divine Presence

340 Dwelling in the Past

341 Physical Health

342 Shifting Gears

343 Mental Energy

344 Sense of Safety

345 Conscious Cooking

346 With Thanks

347 Grace

348 Time Management

349 Giving and Receiving

350 Processing New Information

351 Gender and Gender Identity

352 Step Up, Step Back

353 Different Ways to Rest

354 Alleviating Suffering

355 Ancient Water

356 Courage

357 Back in Time to Love Yourself as an Adult

358 Anticipation

359 Miracles

360 Abundance

361 Planning for the
     Down Slope
362 Center/Within
363 Open Guidance

364 Remembering
365 Imagining Your
     Dream to Life

Appendix: Expanding Your Practice • 407

   Invocation: Welcoming the Spirits and Directions • 407

   Ceremonies and Rituals • 409

   Deeper Experiences • 414

   Moon Ceremonies and Journeys • 425

   Solstices and Equinoxes: Ceremonies and Journeys • 428

FAQ • 437

Notes • 440

Acknowledgments • 447

Resources • 448

SHAMANISM
FOR
EVERY DAY

365 Journeys

Coming Home

S TEPPING OUTSIDE, feeling the soft moss under my feet, I instantly felt lighter—relieved somehow of a burden I didn't even realize I'd been carrying. Cool air moved past, calming my skin and drawing a gentle clacking, like wind chimes, from the bamboo grove nearby. White flowers floated in a warm volcanic rock pool, releasing their sweet fragrance as I slipped in. The blue of the ocean was a distant shimmer. The blue of the sky reflected in the surface of the pool. I floated in the water, relaxed and lost in my own thoughts.

A tiger emerged from the shade of the bamboo and glided into the pool. Her eyes were intent on me. Paddling silently, her powerful shoulders flexed as she sliced the surface. Water soaked her dense fur. The delicate pink of her tongue contrasted with the dark cavern of her mouth. Impossibly fast, she was upon me. She reached an enormous paw around my neck and pulled me close. We tussled playfully for a moment, then settled back and relaxed into the water. It was good to see her again.

Yes, this did happen to me. It happens quite often, actually, but not in my waking life. It happens when I journey.

Before I began practicing shamanism, when I was quite young, tigers visited me in meditation. Extraordinary realms are available when we shift our state of consciousness. Compassionate spiritual helpers arrive to assist us as we navigate life. These meetings can occur in a variety of ways, such as through deep prayer, the dream state, meditation, and sometimes even spontaneously, yet the most profound and consistent way I've found of accessing those places and beings is shamanic journeying.

I was introduced to the formal practice of shamanic journeying in my 20s. It was a cool fall day on a grassy slope in New England. I was accompanied by my mother and grandmother, and a small group of special women. A dear friend gave instructions for how to seek a power animal. Then she drummed. I had no expectations, and what happened next amazed me. I met that exquisite tiger, who I had seen before in meditations, but this experience was richer and more interactive. I felt like I was coming home. I immediately began journeying regularly, exploring new places and meeting many extraordinary helping spirits.

This practice has made an astonishing difference in my life. Prior to this time, it felt like something was just out of reach; the nature of reality eluded me somehow, leaving me unsatisfied in a way I couldn't verbalize or understand. When I spent time in nature or created art, I inched closer to this elusive something, but when I journeyed, my world expanded magnificently. That "coming home" feeling evolved over time. The sense of wonder is still here; new places, beings, and insights are revealed regularly, often with a sense of familiarity similar to that first journey, like a memory I've forgotten. These places and beings are treasured counterparts to my physical home places and beloved people, animals, and plants. When times are good, I celebrate with them; when times are difficult, I seek solace and guidance from them. These spirits are my family; these places are my home.

Connecting with spirit and nature, as shamans do, often conjures images of wild, remote places—Amazonian rainforests, high desert mesas, and Mongolian steppes. While there can be great value in the spiritual experiences unique to those places, shamanic practice is about the here and now. *Your* here and now. If you're like me, that here and now is usually less dramatically wild and more subtly beautiful. I see my neighbors' rooftops while watching the wildlife. I notice violets blooming as I take out the trash. I connect with the spirits with whom I share this land, in all their varied forms. As with most relationships, the more loving time spent, the deeper the relationships become. Practicing shamanism from your backyard can be rich and meaningful. There is exquisite beauty and wisdom in the "home" of our bodies and the everyday spaces we inhabit. Ironically, even during periods when I have a hyperlocal focus I feel more connected to the planet as a whole. The roots of relationships formed here have an expansive reach.

Find your true power and connection to spirit by putting down roots wherever you are—in the city, on a farm, or in a suburban backyard. Unfurl your tendrils to sense and deepen your relationship to the spirits of place and to the elements around and within you. If you nurture those relationships, through observation and conscious interaction, you develop the reciprocity you need to create health and equilibrium now and in the future.

Our most powerful connections to spiritual wisdom and healing reside at home, metaphorically and literally. Paradoxically, as we recognize the vast impacts of our global, ecological, and personal interconnectedness, the implications of coming home become increasingly important. Our relationships with ourselves, community, nature, and spirit dwell in the core spaces of home and our local environments. An appreciation of our interconnection and a local focus are fundamental aspects of shamanism. Sustaining equilibrium within ourselves and with one another takes consistent effort. Shamanism provides us with effective, time-tested practices for creating and maintaining personal and collective balance and transformation. Authentic power does not reside only in certain places or with certain people. The more we understand the interconnectedness of all things, the more we realize our sources of spiritual wisdom and healing are available from anywhere and at any time. That place is here. That time is now.

Why I Created
Shamanism for Every Day: 365 Journeys

We live in intense times. The pressures of daily life can leave us emotionally, mentally, physically, and spiritually depleted. Shamanic journeying can enable us to rejuvenate, reconnect to wisdom, and restore health, despite those pressures. I hope the journeys I provide in this book make the process of developing a daily practice in shamanic journeying easier.

There are many paths to the divine and many methods to access sound spiritual advice. These journey topics can be used for prayer and contemplation. My helping spirits come to me both in meditations and in shamanic journeys. The method is not as important as making the space in our lives to connect purposely to the divine within us and the helping spirits we coexist with, not only for our personal healing and evolution, but also for the healing and evolution of our world. While this is a shamanic book, because that is my primary path, the daily journeys contained within are adaptable to your own spiritual practice.

A daily practice is powerful. I believe it is crucial for our health and well-being. Those who know me know I am not a purist when it comes to what form this takes. "Practice" can mean many different things. I love the classic quote from the Dalai Lama: "My religion is very simple. My religion is kindness." However, I think we also need to be honest with ourselves about what it takes for true transformation. Checking the box on a brief journey or meditation each day is probably not going to cut it. The daily practice is the gateway; it's the beginning.

Our times call for a genuine depth of personal work and outward action for true evolution to occur. A trap we can fall into is to dabble in practices and become disillusioned when we don't have immediate transformation. Or to think that because we had a few profound experiences we are now enlightened. Or to forget that life is our primary spiritual practice. Although we talk about ordinary life and spiritual life, ordinary reality and non-ordinary reality, regular states of consciousness and shifted states of consciousness, it is really all one thing. This is life. We are, and always have been, on a spiritual journey together.

How to Use
Shamanism for Every Day: 365 Journeys

This book can be used in many ways: as a daily shamanic guide, a resource for drumming circles, a daily meditation, and as an inspirational seed for a spiritual support group. The guidance you receive from using the topics in *Shamanism for Every Day: 365 Journeys* is intended to enhance your sense of well-being, support your practice, and help you stay connected to your own sources of wisdom and intuition.

If you practice shamanism, you may want to use drumming while you journey. Music or silence are also perfectly fine. My preference is to journey in the morning, while others I know like to use a journey as a reading at night to plant a seed for the next day. Experiment and see what works for you. We will review the practice of shamanic journeying in more depth a little further on.

You can also use the daily suggestions as meditations. Incorporate them into your existing practice, or, if you are new to meditation, perhaps spend a few moments following your breath in and out, gently observing your thoughts, and intentionally relaxing your physical body. When you feel ready, state the daily suggestion and observe what your innate wisdom reveals to you. Notice the sensations, thoughts, and images that arise; let information well up without judgment. When you are finished with your meditation, take some notes about the experience to remember and review later.

You can simply contemplate each topic at the start of your day. Then, as your day evolves, notice how the theme relates to and supports your thinking and guides your choices. Prayer is another meaningful way to work with the topics. Feel free to reword topics to suit your religious or personal belief system.

Pay attention to recurring themes

Some themes are worthy of regular attention and you will see them recur frequently. They can be important to a routine of spiritual self-care, rather than a one-time exploration. These recurring topics include:

- Love
- Kindness
- Engaging nature
- Rest
- Receiving open guidance
- Working with the elements
- Play and lightness
- Silence
- Dreaming/visioning
- How to best use time and energy

Perform ceremonies and rituals

In these daily journeys, I often suggest asking for and performing a ritual or ceremony. These can be done in ordinary reality or non-ordinary reality, or a combination of both. "Ordinary" reality is our everyday waking consciousness. "Non-ordinary" reality, or the "shamanic state of consciousness," is the spirit world that we perceive when journeying. I think our waking life can be pretty extraordinary, but the distinction is helpful. Meaningful ceremonies can be very simple; the power is in the intention, focus, and energy that you put into them. An elaborate ceremony done by rote in a distracted state is less powerful than a simple, short one done with reverence and concentration. If this is new for you, don't worry. Be yourself, do a bit of preparation, and show up fully. There is a fuller description of designing your own ceremonies in the Appendix: "Ceremonies and Rituals" at the end of the book.

Be light

Under no circumstances should this book become a burden to you! These journeys are not things to add to a to-do list. Please don't feel guilty if you miss days. I wrote *Shamanism for Every Day* to support you and give you interesting ideas to work with. If you don't connect with the topic, don't do it. Make up your own, skip days, or use the book out of order if you prefer. I hope you will treat it more like a caring friend who has your back than a demanding professor to whom you feel accountable. There are some deep topics contained inside; some may be outside your comfort zone, others are meant to be calming or playful. We can always journey to ask for something, but we never know what the spirits are going to give us. Relax, go lightly, and enjoy your journeys.

What Is Shamanism?

*What's really important about shamanism is that
there is another reality that you can
personally discover . . . we are not alone.*

—MICHAEL HARNER

SHAMANISM IS A SYSTEM of direct revelation. What we currently refer to as shamanism is complex, nuanced, and incredibly old; however, when distilled to its defining essence, shamanism is about a practical and personal relationship to the spiritual. It is from this perspective that we explore shamanic practice in *Shamanism for Every Day: 365 Journeys*. I love that there is no dogma in this work. There is a structure to work from, an ancient foundation upon which you can grow your own practice organically, but you don't have to believe anything that I, or anyone else, tells you. Each person has their own experience of the divine and the spiritual world around them. Through an intentional practice of shamanism, those experiences help you determine how to stay healthy and content, how to relate to others in the most positive way, and how to create a life you're passionate about.

A contemporary discussion about shamanism would not be complete without acknowledging some brutal history. As indigenous peoples' spiritual traditions have existed across the globe, so too have the vicious and systemic attempts to eradicate them. "Western" cultures have consistently and methodically used physical, legal, and cultural violence to eliminate people, languages, healing knowledge, spiritual ceremonies, and access to sacred land. In some places, and in very recent times, that tide has turned. Interest in shamanic practice is part of that shift. For those of us who are practicing freely today, in any culture, it's important to remember that we do so only because of those who have come before and preserved shamanic traditions.

The word "shaman" comes from "*šaman*" in the Tungus language spoken by the Evenki people of Siberia. Many other cultures have their own words for the person who fulfills the role of the shaman, including *angakok* (Inuit of the Arctic regions), *mudang* (Korea), *znakharka* (Ukraine), *p'aqo* (Andean/Quecha of South America), *kami* (Mongolia), *sukya* (Miskito and Sumu of Honduras and Nicaragua), *sangoma* (South Africa), *táltos* (Hungary), *dukun* (Indonesia), and *wu* (China). Traditionally, shamans have responsibilities that are similar to those of doctors, counselors, priests, and seers. Shamans straddle two worlds: the spiritual realm and ordinary reality. They need to be skilled navigators of both, understanding the rules of each and knowing how to move back and forth between them. We can think of it somewhat like people who move between cultures frequently for business or family reasons. The person who travels back and forth between places needs a basic understanding of both languages, the rules and local customs, and ways of getting around.

Anthropologists adopted the word "shamanism" as an umbrella term for a collective of beliefs and practices. Some of these core principles and practices include ideas about cosmology, working with helping spirits, how illness occurs and is healed, the interconnectedness of all things in the natural world, our relationship to time (and those who came before us and will come next), expanded perception, the intentional shifting of consciousness (especially through the use of percussion), and specific methods for working with the spiritual realms to stay in balance individually and collectively. Different cultures have distinctive beliefs and practices. We will focus on the aspects that are more globally consistent.

Shamanism is the oldest spiritual practice on the planet. It has been part of society on six continents. We know from archaeological evidence that the practice dates back at least 40,000 years. Indigenous knowledge is not always easy to translate into Western concepts of self, others, nature, and relationship. Historically, this knowledge came from personal observation and the collective transmission from generation to generation through oral traditions of storytelling, ceremony, medicine, cosmology, dance, and art. These indigenous or shamanic ways of being in the world were not adjunct explorations, but integral parts of society and survival for our ancestors.

Shamanism has survived for so long (with its many names) because it evolves and adapts to its place and time. It stays relevant because it is always happening; it doesn't fossilize, it doesn't become codified into a bureaucracy or institution. Shamanists are rooted first within their current place and space. Direct revelation is not about emulating the customs of a particular people or a particular time. It is about your *own* experience in your *own* place and time. It is about your relationship with helping spirits, with the spirits of the place you are in, and with your relationship to your own inner divinity, right here, right now.

While we are situated within our own relationship to the spiritual world, our specific spot in the web of all life, our tree trunk in the forest community, we are also connected to everything else that exists. This idea of interconnectivity is fundamental to the experience of shamanism. From our place on the web, filaments connect us to all others. Our trunk is our own, and the roots that go deep into the soil connect us to ancient times and ancient beings, as do the branches that reach up into the heavens. While keeping our attention on shamanism as an individual practice, we still want to ground it within the context of a universal experience with access to a vast realm of knowledge that pushes the boundaries of commonly held beliefs of time and physicality. Much of the wisdom of shamanic systems is bearing out in areas of cutting-edge science today. Physicists are positing and proving that time does not move in as clear-cut a linear progression as we once believed. Emerging fields like epigenetics are exploring the effects of ancestral trauma and traits being passed down generationally. Concepts like non-local healing and one-mind consciousness fall squarely into the category of shamanic beliefs shared cross-culturally for tens of thousands of years. When we practice shamanism (or any spiritual tradition), we tap into its history. When we develop a deeply personal relationship with the sacred, we help evolve our collective relationship to it as well. Living in alignment with shamanic principles encompasses much more than the practice of journeying, but journeying is a powerful step toward creating meaningful relationships with the spirit within and around us. If this is your first experience journeying, I'm excited to share this gift with you. If you've been on this path a long time, thank you for walking a while with me.

How to Journey

*Shamanic journeying is a joyful path to regaining
the knowledge of how to bring our lives back to
a place of harmony and balance.*

—SANDRA INGERMAN

ANY SINCERE PERSON who is willing to practice can learn shamanic journeying. We can all access the wisdom of our ancestors, reach out to compassionate spirits who are willing to reach back to us, here and now, in our present time. We urgently need that wisdom, individually and collectively.

———— ∞ ————

I ask a few things from you to start, and then we will map out the steps to take a journey.

1. *If possible, find a human teacher to help guide you in this work.* Ultimately, your helping spirits will be your primary teachers, but having someone who has walked this path before you can be invaluable. It is also a teacher's responsibility to create a spiritually secure space, forming a strong container for the work. Visit WholeSpirit.com for more information about learning in person and online.

2. *Keep your head on straight.* If, in your first journey, you meet a spirit who tells you to leave your spouse, sell all your belongings, and move onto a boat, think again. Developing trusted relationships over time, learning how to interpret the guidance you are given in a journey, and balancing that information with your own reflections, emotions, and research, are all important to practicing in a grounded way. These messages are specific for you as an individual, so looking to standardized interpretations falls short. The guidance may not necessarily be wrong in the long run, but don't be rash. Ask for additional input, and don't take orders from someone you don't know yet.

3. *Toss out your preconceptions.* You may have an idea about what journeying will be like, but the odds are you're going to be surprised; it will be both easier and harder, more visual and less visual. You will receive clearer, more profound information than you ever imagined, your spirits will be more obtuse and frustrating than you thought possible, they will make you laugh, they will make you cry, you will be bored and elated. You just won't know until you establish your practice, and even *then*, it's amazing how astonishing it can be. Over time you may see journeys that pick up in *exactly* the spot where you left off years ago, you will remember a helping spirit you knew as a child and had forgotten for decades, or you'll have a visitation that changes everything. Sometimes there is silence. And you don't get to pick your helping

spirits; they pick you. Clear your mind as much as possible before you go and just show up.

Why Journey?

The practice of shamanism is a profound and direct way to connect to your spiritual power. This occurs through your relationship with and assistance from compassionate spirits who are willing to help you, and through a rekindling of your connection to your own spirit. Journeying is a method of shamanic practice, it is not the practice itself. The essence of this work is much more expansive and wondrous. Journeying is a way to open the door to the incredible world of spirit that is all around us, a world that many of us have lost the ability to perceive and engage with. You may choose to walk through that door, straddle the threshold, or just crack it open a bit periodically.

Exploring this way of living and interacting with the world is up to you. The support will be there as you need it. How you foster and channel your personal power is up to you. Other people on this path can be companions and guides for you. The ultimate teachers will come from the spirit realm. By developing strong relationships with these spirits, while staying connected and true to your inner divinity, you create a link to the divine knowledge of shamanic traditions throughout the ages.

Helping Spirits

At the heart of shamanic practice is our relationship to helping spirits. Developing a strong, consistent connection to one or more compassionate spirits is the starting point. These spirits take many forms, including human, animal, plant, even gods or goddesses that we are familiar with from mythology. I think of the spiritual beings who are willing to develop meaningful and sustained relationship with us as our *personal pantheon*. Akin to your network of family, friends, mentors, and teachers in ordinary reality, your personal pantheon is a network of loving beings whom you connect with in non-ordinary reality.

The beings we meet in spirit, just like those we meet in body, are individuals. The dolphin that comes to you in your journeys is likely not the same one that comes to me in mine. Although it may be tempting to dash to a "What Does Your Spirit Animal Mean" website or book, that will give you only a partial sense of why that animal may be showing up for you. It's better to develop your personal relationship, ask *your* dolphin, share with *your* dolphin, be with *your* dolphin. If you were introduced to someone special a friend thought you should meet, would your first thought be, *What does this person "mean?"* Probably not. Maybe something more like: *Who are they? What are they like? What do they have to share with me? How can I have a good relationship with them?* Spirits are specific beings, and when we relate to them with that in mind, our connections are deeper.

Helping spirits can come to us in clear and vivid ways, breaking through the veil between ordinary and non-ordinary reality. We go to them in our journeys. The deeper reality is more holistic, in that we coexist, neither coming nor going but being together always. But since we are used to functioning as individuals oriented to place and time, it's helpful to have some clear directions and rituals for connecting consistently.

Journeying provides a pathway for us to follow to the worlds of pure spirit, and for our helping spirits to help us here. In many cosmologies, and in the practice of core shamanism,* the world is divided into three layers, an Upper, Middle, and Lower World. The Upper and Lower Worlds are similar in that they are entirely spiritual. They do not have physical form. They have nothing to do with religious ideas of heaven and hell, and everything to do with which way we travel to reach them. The Middle World is where we live, this beautiful intersection of form and spirit. There are helping spirits in the Middle World, too, and as this is a complicated physical world it is also a complicated spiritual world. We begin our explorations in the lower and upper realms. Once you've developed a trusting relationship with a helping spirit over time, ask them to come along as a guide as you travel further into these realms.

A belief in the existence of helping spirits does not contradict a belief in the existence of a more all-encompassing

---

* Core shamanism is a concept developed by Michael Harner, an anthropologist and founder of the Foundation for Shamanic Studies. According to the FSS, core shamanism is the "universal, near-universal, and common features of shamanism, together with journeys to other worlds, a distinguishing feature of shamanism . . . the principles of core shamanism are not bound to any specific cultural group or perspective."

divinity, what we might call God, Spirit, or Universal Consciousness. We can relate to our helping spirits and honor them as we might our revered elders without worshipping them. Again, shamanism is a practice of direct experience. Your practice may include other faiths, if you choose. My mother is Christian and a shamanist. My grandmother was Jewish and a shamanist. They were able to embrace the beauty of shamanism alongside the beauty of those faiths. Not only is shamanic practice compatible with other spiritual traditions, there are elements of shamanism embodied within other spiritual traditions. Catholic theologian Leonardo Boff connects the shamanic belief that everything in nature is animated by a cosmic spiritual force to the Biblical description of *ruah*, "the energy of nature." Contemporary rabbi Gershon Winkler reflects on the ancient origins of Jewish practice, "Our visionaries came not from rabbinical seminaries and academies of higher learning but from solitary walkabouts and vision quests. . . . They were masters of sorcery and shamanism, dancing comfortably between the realms of spirit and matter, celebrating the magic of the worlds around them and beyond them. They knew the language of the trees, the grasses, the frogs . . . They followed rivers to discover truths, and climbed mountains to liberate their spirits."

Drumming

In order to see the spiritual world that is the foundation of the visible world, shamans shift their state of consciousness. Part of that shift in vision occurs due to the drumming that underlies the journey. Monotonous percussion sound, known as "sonic driving," is the most common method used across cultures for entering this altered state. Scientists have learned that specific rhythms alter brain waves. In a study among the Salish of the Northwest Coast of North America, shamanic drumming created a shift to the theta wave EEG frequency (4–7 cycles/second), which is closely associated with hypnotic, dream, and deeply meditative states. This form of drumming can induce powerful experiences. Michael Harner states, "After having personally practiced shamanism, shamanic healing, and shamanic journeying for more than half a century, I can say that there is nothing I have encountered in reports of the spiritual experiences of saints, prophets, psychedelic drug experimenters, near death survivors, avatars and other mystics that is not commonly experienced when following classic journey methods using a drum."

In the beginning, most people find it helpful to either have someone else drum or to work with recorded drumming. You can try drumming for yourself, but it usually takes some practice to master. Make sure whatever drum track you use has a "call back." This is a series of fast beats that will let you know when it is time to retrace your steps and return from your journey. It is a good idea to listen to the track you plan to use *without* journeying to it first—just so you have no surprises. I once bought an ocean sounds track specifically for the sound of the waves. I was pretty deep into a meditation when a gull screeched loudly and I practically jumped out of my skin! Gulls are a part of the ocean environment, so I couldn't be upset, but it was not the auditory experience I was going for.

If you are using a drumming track, have it ready. If not, decide in advance how long your journey is going to be and have a clear call back to return you to ordinary reality. While this is usually built in to a shamanic drumming track, if you are journeying to music or silence, perhaps set a very gentle chime to help you know when it is time to return. Make sure you are clear on the steps for a safe, grounded shamanic journey before you head out.

Mindset

Before you even begin the practical steps of your journeys, there are some internal steps you can take to make them more successful: Have an open mind about the possibilities, manage your expectations, address any concerns you have, and try not to judge your experience while you are having it.

The rules of ordinary reality and non-ordinary reality are different. You are probably quite used to the rules of ordinary reality at this point; gravity keeping you anchored to wherever you are sitting or standing, staying a consistent size in relation to your surroundings, time moving forward, people and animals remaining people and animals respectively. These are not-so-minor details of living that we tend to take for granted because they are consistent. You may not know yet what non-ordinary reality will be like for you, so have an open mind and experiment. Perhaps you will be able to use non-ordinary-reality rules to solve problems in new ways. If you find yourself facing a situation that seems impossible to resolve in a journey, consider solutions outside the rules of the reality you live in every day. Be creative. Ask for help. Perhaps in your journeying state you can change your size, or make light appear if you need it, or move faster than you can in ordinary reality.

Which of your senses are most active in your journeys will likely vary. Some people are more visual, some more auditory or multisensory. One student of mine was having a little trouble in the beginning of class because she didn't feel like she was seeing much. However, she was receiving information directly through her body. Her body was vibrating and she was experiencing different sensations when she asked questions in her journeys. She became more accepting of her kinesthetic sense as valid and her journeys became more enriching. We are a visual culture, so we often expect journeys to be like movies that start when we close our eyes. We also want clearly worded answers that fully explain the questions gnawing at our souls. Maybe you will get some of these, but often answers are given in images and symbols, scenes that play out before us, or in other rich and varied ways that we have to work to interpret. We're babies in the scheme of things spiritually, yet the helping spirits rarely spoon-feed us. They love us, and give us what we need, but not always what we want or expect.

If you are concerned about journeying for any reason, voice your apprehension. The more you bring it up and out, the more it can dissipate. People commonly wonder things like: What if nothing happens, What if I don't remember the way back, What if I don't meet a helping spirit, and What if I don't like drumming? I will answer some of these concerns in the "FAQ" section in the Appendix. A balanced mindset is one that sits between openness and discernment. This work may take some trust to start. Approaching with a sense of gratitude and appreciation for the mystery helps. Consider that you are greater than you know, and so are the ways in which we all connect with the seen and unseen. Be open to possibilities. And remember, you are a sovereign being who is allowed to set boundaries and define your own comfort zone. You have discernment and choice. If you decide to end your journey early, simply retrace your steps and come back. If you feel uncomfortable in a situation, you can leave it. This work can push up against our edges a bit for sure, and that is where transformation happens. Hopefully, you will not shy away from an experience simply because it's new or different, or maybe even a little difficult. This is different from feeling in your gut that something is not right for you. Listen to your instincts, in your ordinary life and in your shamanic journeys. You are allowed to say no thank you, or yes please. Set boundaries that feel right to you.

Before deciding to join one of my journeying classes, one student expressed some concern about losing control while in the journey state. One of the many benefits of using drumming or some other form of percussion is that you shift your state of consciousness while retaining a dual awareness of your surroundings. As many people know, hallucinogenic plants and fungi have a long, rich history in shamanic ceremony and healing. They have benefits, including both clinical and spiritual applications, many of which are documented scientifically through universities and research facilities. However, it is significantly harder to come back from a journey at will if that journey involves peyote, for example, than if it just involves drumming. Additionally, drumming is universally legal.

Know what may hold you back as far as mindset. If there are things that you're especially nervous about, try to address them early so they don't get in your way. This is where an accessible human teacher is such an asset. Sometimes our fears can be easily addressed and fade away; sometimes they are more tangled, and we need support as we proceed more slowly or follow tips about trying deviations from the standard methods.

For most people, creating a healthy mindset is less about managing fear and more about dealing with our distractible and judgmental selves. Be gentle with yourself. Don't worry about getting it just right. If you fall asleep, or forget something that happened, or aren't sure if you made something up, it's okay. In the place and time that we live we have become accustomed to distractions and multitasking. As much as you can, let yourself have your experiences and save the analysis for later. Let journeying be an adventure rather than something to master.

Setting the Stage

Before starting your journey, remember to set your space. Settle in a quiet spot where you won't be disturbed. Wear cozy clothes and have anything else you need to feel comfortable and relaxed—but not so comfortable that you fall asleep! Take as long as you need to transition from your ordinary activities and headspace to this intentional one. Although seeing with shaman's eyes is something we can practice in our ordinary lives, it often takes some deliberate action to prepare to make the shift to a journeying state.

For some people, the setting in which they journey

strongly affects the kind of experience they have, for others, not as much. If you're not sure which category you fall into (or if you are somewhere in between), you may want to experiment. If your setting is very impactful to you, be especially deliberate in how you tend to your internal and external space before you journey.

Transitioning from your everyday tasks creates an environment conducive to the journeying state. Depending on your temperament, this may take a few moments or a longer time. A calming process may be most helpful for you to get into a journeying state of mind. Lighting a candle, burning some sage, and having a warm bath may help you let go of the thoughts of the day and turn inward toward this practice. Conversely, you may prefer dancing or chanting to move energy through your body and build power in preparation for your journey. Choose some act or symbolic gesture that will signal to your subconscious that you are preparing for this journey to meet a compassionate spiritual guide.

Perhaps spend a few moments doing some deep breathing, drum, sing, dance, watch the movement of the leaves in the trees or the birds outside. Do something to delineate and honor that you are about to shift from an ordinary to a non-ordinary state of consciousness. Don't rush it.

You may also want to investigate the best times of day for you to journey. If you are naturally a morning person, that may be an ideal time; but if you are fighting sleep or feeling anxious about getting to work on time, later in the day may be better for you.

Asking Questions

Coming up with questions may sound easy but can be one of the most challenging parts of the process, and it's very important. This is one of the reasons I compiled this collection of journeys. I wanted you to have some readily available, concisely worded journey topics. Of course, you should journey on your personal questions as well. Or leave things open. I start many days by asking my helping spirits: "What do I need to know today?" or "Please show me what needs to be seen." I also ask for guidance about specific things, and sometimes journey simply to say "thank you."

Whether you are going with a very specific question or a more spacious intention, the support available to us from this form of spiritual dialogue and relationship is a treasure, a source for wisdom and advice with incredible depth and breadth. If you are journeying on a specific subject, knowing what you're *really* asking, and formulating that into a concise question, is a bit of an art in itself. It's not hard once you remember a few guidelines, and the process of fine-tuning the question can also help you clarify what you truly want guidance about.

Write down a concise question before you journey

Formulate concise questions to ask your helping spirits. On one level we are going to get what the spirits decide to give when we journey, and what they think we need to hear may override what we are asking about on a given day. However, having a clear question to start helps avoid misinterpretation of the answer. Two-part questions aren't ideal, especially early on. Once you have some practice, you can ask a follow-up without having to take a full second journey. Write down your question and read it back to yourself. Pretend you don't have any inside information about the issue. Does it make sense? Memorize it so that you ask it the same way once you are in your journey.

Avoid asking yes/no or should/shouldn't questions. This minimizes your personal power and agency, rather than allowing you to gather information and then make your own decisions. Asking binary questions robs you of an opportunity to gather data and can result in completely unexpected and unintentional results. Usually, yes-or-no questions contain many underlying assumptions. For example, "Should I move to Hawaii?" Implied in that may be: Will I enjoy living in Hawaii? Will I be able to find a job in Hawaii? Will I meet my soul mate in Hawaii? So ask what you *really* mean. Perhaps there is a life lesson that can be learned hard and fast in Hawaii, maybe it will be so much fun and you will also go bankrupt, or have your heart broken, or get stuck in a hurricane. Those experiences may be valuable to you in the big picture, and your helping spirits may think they would be useful, but I would say it's better to ask something like, "What would it feel like to live in Hawaii now?" Remember that spirits may have different definitions of "good for you."

How, who, where, why, and *what* questions are more useful. *When* is a little tricky. Spirits exist outside of our perceptions of time and space. When we journey we are sharing in that somewhat, which is why a fifteen-minute journey in ordinary time can feel like two minutes or two hours in non-ordinary time. Ask a *when* question if you like, but know that "soon" to a spirit may not be so soon to you.

Respect the privacy of others

Don't invade someone else's privacy. We know we shouldn't snoop in ordinary reality, so don't do it in non-ordinary reality, either.

Practice interpreting everything in your journeys

The language of the spirits is often metaphorical. Paying attention to the many different ways that your journey can be interpreted in relation to your question is part of the challenge, and part of the enjoyment, of this practice. Everything can relate: what the environment looks like, ambient sounds, direct spoken communication, things you are shown, places you are taken, the way your body feels, internal knowing—all these aspects can be fodder for compiling an answer to your question.

Use sound judgment

Honing your interpreting skills, and putting them to the test over time, helps you get better at understanding what your helping spirits are trying to convey to you. And of course, always incorporate other methods of decision-making, like intuition, instincts, logic, and research, before making vital decisions.

Don't work beyond your training

In addition to seeking guidance, shamans and shamanic practitioners also enter the spirit world to ask for healing. When working for yourself, you can ask your spirit allies for what is for your highest good. Seek medical and psychological care as needed; the healing journey is analogous to intercessory prayer. However, doing shamanic healing work for someone else is different. It is beyond the scope of this book, and requires training and, very importantly, permission. Please keep in mind what your level of experience is and what you can ethically do for others in this realm.

Departing

As I mentioned, it's important to be aware of what world you are in when journeying. Shamans can move effectively between worlds, and indeed most helping spirits are not confined to one world or the other; however, it is important to know when your journeys start and stop. It would be unsafe to walk around in ordinary reality while operating under the rules of non-ordinary reality. One of the many things I appreciate about this practice is that there are clear steps to follow, an order and system for navigating. This structure allows for free exploration of fantastic realms, but we don't usually journey just to wander around aimlessly. Although there are times that are less structured, like spending sweet quality time with helping spirits, or being in a state of gratitude while in a favorite place in non-ordinary reality, shamans typically journey to ask for information (divination) or to perform healings. Framing journeys with a clear return to ordinary reality helps keep us grounded after our travels.

You will need to pick a place in ordinary reality from which to begin your journeys and to which you return at the end. This should be a place that you have actually been to in real life, not a dream place, or a place you go in meditation. It's okay if it's a place from childhood. It should be a place in nature that feels comfortable to you. Ideally, it's special in some way, but it doesn't have to be. Don't worry too much about picking the perfect place the first time. You can always change the place you choose with your next journey. Not surprisingly, the kind of place that works best will depend on whether you are traveling to the Lower or Upper World. Over time, you will likely develop well-worn paths to these realms and specific places where you often meet certain spirits. If you are setting out to have a conversation with someone in particular, you'll go to where they are, Upper or Lower. Sometimes it's not that clear which spirit will show up at a given time or for a given question, so it's also fine to see which world you are drawn to and then go. Ultimately, we create some processes that we do routinely so we don't have to think about the mechanics, and then we turn it over to our helping spirits. Once you've done it a bit, there will be variations on how your helping spirits show up (within journeys and outside of them); some are quite extraordinary.

Descending to the Lower World

When journeying to the Lower World, your departure place should be a place in nature where you can experience yourself moving down into the Earth. Tree roots, animal burrows, caves, and natural springs are generally good places. It's fine to use a little imagination. Make sure you envision yourself moving downward, not horizontally. Once you have experienced yourself at your departure place—and this is true no matter where you plan to journey—hold your intention clearly and firmly in your mind.

If this is your first journey, your intention is to go to the Lower World to meet a power animal. If you already have a power animal but need guidance about divination journeys, read the steps below as a refresher. If you are an experienced journeyer, you can skip to the "Daily Journeys" section now.

Before you take your first journey, read all the steps below: As the drumming begins . . .

- Hold your intention clearly in your mind. If this is your first journey, your intention is: *I am going to the Lower World to meet my power animal.*

- Envision yourself moving from your departure place down into a tunnel or passageway into the Earth.

- Move downward through the tunnel until you discern that you have come out of it. It is important to mark this transition in some way, because it indicates you have moved from the Middle to the Lower World. You may *see* the tunnel ending, you may *feel* it because the quality of the air shifts, you may know It happens because it *smells* different. Mark the transition and make sure you go into and out of this downward passageway.

31

- When you emerge from the tunnel, if your helping spirit is waiting there, off you go! What comes next depends on where you are in the process. If you have never met this particular spirit before, simply see what they are like. How do they communicate with you? What does it feel like to be in their presence? Maybe ask if they are your power animal. In a subsequent journey, perhaps ask if they are willing to answer a question for you. If you are familiar with this spirit, now may be the time to greet them and then share the purpose of this journey.

- If you come out of the tunnel and there is not a spirit waiting for you, state your intention again, and begin to explore. You may find a power animal elsewhere, or later in the journey. If not, simply explore the Lower World.

- When you hear the call back beat, say thank you. Retrace your steps, come back up the tunnel, and return to your departure place.

Ascending to the Upper World

When journeying to the Upper World, your departure place should naturally be a place from which you can move upward. Treetops, mountaintops, mesas, and cliffs are possibilities. Again, choose a place that you know from your waking life. Once you've prepared yourself and your environment, settle in and relax. Often, an intention for a first journey to the Upper World is to ask to meet a spirit teacher in human form. Hold your intention firmly in your mind. Once you are ready, begin the drumming.

- Experience yourself moving upward from your departure place. If you need assistance moving vertically, use a little imagination or ask for help.

- Continue until you pass through a cloudy or misty layer. This layer separates the Middle World from the Upper World.

- In the Upper World, experience being with a teacher. Get to know their communication style, what power they embody, and what it feels like to be near them.

- If you do not meet a spirit teacher on this journey, explore the Upper World and become familiar with this place.

- When you hear the call back beat, say thank you. Retrace your steps, come back down through the misty layer, and return to your departure place.

Moving Out to the Middle World

We live in the Middle World. The Middle World is comprised of spirit and matter, the Upper and Lower Worlds are only spirit. The Middle World is a place of nature, of air and earth, of wind and fire, of plants and animals and minerals. It is a place of linear time. We can encounter many kinds of spirits in the Middle World, and want even more discernment with our interactions. As our lives are beautiful and sometimes complicated, so is the Middle World.

Journeying to the Middle World is very simple, because you are already here—just walk on out. Prepare yourself as you would for any journey (setting the stage, shifting your state of consciousness, formulating your intention, etc.). Instead of using a departure place as you would in going to the Lower or Upper World, simply envision yourself moving out from where you are. Your place in physical reality is your starting point. From there you can connect with the trees in your yard, the spirits of the land, the elements themselves, or travel over long distances in short periods of time. Shamans traditionally ventured out in the Middle World to understand what was happening around them, like finding where food and water were located.

The Middle World has some added layers of complexity that go deeper than we have time to delve into here. Often in core shamanism, students are taught to start with the Upper and Lower Worlds because there is more clarity about the *kinds* of spirits you will meet there. While I agree with this, I don't steer people away from Middle World journeys, because the Middle World is incredible! Sometimes we need to do a little more investigating about spirits we encounter in the Middle World, especially those that have a human form. If you are starting a practice, begin by developing a strong bond with helping spirits that you meet in the Upper and Lower Worlds. Ask them to accompany you on your journeys, especially for your early Middle World adventures. In general, it is always a good idea to ask a trusted helping spirit to be with you while journeying.

Returning and Integrating

Once you have returned, take a moment to gather yourself. The transitions between states of consciousness are important; a smooth return allows you to capture insights and experiences, while an abrupt landing can be disorienting. Document your journey in some way. Write it down in a notebook or make an audio recording. This "immortalizing" honors the time spent and the information given. The shift in consciousness that accompanies the drumming is a move toward the delta brain wave state, which can be very deep and dreamlike. When you come back, you snap back into the beta or alpha brain wave state—a waking or lightly relaxed state—and different kinds of mental processing take over. It's remarkable how easy it is for these rich experiences to wisp away like dreams if you don't capture them, as your mind returns quickly to its usual state of awareness.

At this point, you will probably have some interpreting to do. Sometimes we're given a clear straightforward message or direction; however, the spirit world—like life in general—is rich in symbolism, imagery, and nuance. A journey's meaning may become clear over months or years. Let the information percolate without rushing to conclusions. Journeys can be repeated for clarification, or to go deeper. With repeated journeying you are forming relationships with these other realms. Relationships of any kind are not simply about gathering information. Go and spend time with your helping spirits. Journey to say thank you or to explore. See what changes when you engage your senses in a more expansive way and connect with the spiritual dimensions more intentionally and consistently.

Making Shamanism Part of Every Day

If you are new to this practice, it is likely too early to tell the impact it may have on your life. Like any relationship, any new habit or pattern, any paradigm shift, it takes effort and time. If you only visit your helping spirits when you are in a crisis, are bored, or feel like experimenting, the relationship will only go so far. That dynamic isn't the most fruitful with human relationships, either, although helping spirits are generally more patient with us than our friends or families. Your experiences will not be the same as mine or anyone else's. You decide how you engage. You may be dramatically prompted or called to go further. You may need to stick with it for a while before you feel the power. Although there is no pressure, sporadic engagement doesn't normally lead to a satisfying spiritual practice of any kind.

You don't have to formally journey to "practice" shamanism every day. There are many simple things you can do to incorporate shamanic ways of being into your life. Small changes accumulate over time to become big shifts. Perhaps begin with honoring the sun each morning, thanking your ancestors for your existence, or welcoming your helping spirits to be present with you throughout your day. Perhaps do something in ordinary reality that acknowledges our interconnection, like seeing the people you encounter throughout the day as reflections of spirit, taking steps to reduce your impact on the environment, or being more aware of the power your words have to affect others.

Some of these things are distinctly shamanic, but some are part of many traditions' beliefs about living a spiritually connected and balanced life. Integrating shamanism with your existing spiritual beliefs and practices may be part of creating an authentic practice for who you are, here and now. Learn from others, yet make the work your own. What you decide to share, if anything, about your explorations is up to you. *What's your spirit animal?* has become the subject of online quizzes and pop culture references. Don't mistake that for the sacred thing. For some, the sacredness of these experiences means holding them close as a form of honoring. For others, finding safe places to share and create community is important.

If you have challenges with your journeying practice, see the "FAQ" section in the back of the book or visit WholeSpirit.com for finding help from a teacher.

Daily Journeys

THE FOLLOWING PAGES hold a full year of shamanic exploration. As you embark on your year of journeys, I want to reiterate a few things. The daily journeying suggestions are for you whether you practice shamanism or not. If you practice shamanic journeying, you can go to a compassionate spirit for help with any of the topics. But you can also use these suggestions in meditation to connect with your inner divinity, use them in a mindfulness practice, pray to the divine in one of its many forms, or connect in another way that feels right to you.

Shamanism for Every Day: 365 Journeys is meant to be a support for you, not a burdensome "to do" list item. I wrote it to be a gentle support for you as you walk your spiritual path. Don't let anything turn that presence into pressure. Enjoy the "journey" of your day whether or not it includes this specific practice of working with the journeys in this book. If you miss a day, or many days, that is fine. There is no one looking over your shoulder, no one judging you for sleeping in or deciding to set this aside entirely. You can do the journeys in order or skip around. The table of contents lists the topics that are covered in the book so you can look up the journeys that interest you the most or seem most relevant to where you are on a given day.

I've filled the "Daily Journeys" pages with specific topics to seed your practice. Of course, you should formulate your own questions as often as you wish. Take rest days and gratitude journeys. Some of the most profound and fruitful journeys happen when we simply listen to what the spirits want to tell us. Particularly for those who will use these journeys in order from start to finish, I've distributed some Open Guidance journeys throughout the daily journeys. Space is built in to the year to listen without specific directive. If you are creating your own journey intentions at any point, you can also use the following:

- *What do I need to know today?*
- *Please show me what needs to be seen.*
- *Thank you for providing what is needed.*
- *Please tell me what needs to be heard today*

What will *your* journey be today?

Beginning

*In the beginner's mind there are many possibilities,
in the expert's mind, there are few.*

—SHOSHIN

How do you feel at the start of something new? Excited? Nervous? Do you envision all the wonderful possibilities or all the potential disappointments? When we're at the beginning of something—a relationship, a job, a trip, a project, or even a book or a new course of study—we have a choice. We can focus on the wide array of promising opportunities that our choice has opened or on the ways we might be let down. Where we fall on this spectrum is often based on our past experiences, but the simple choice to begin creates powerful new potential. Much of the time things don't go as planned. Sometimes they go spectacularly awry; other times blessings bloom abundantly and surprisingly out of nowhere. When we approach life with the curious and open mind of a beginner, we prime ourselves for the richest possible menu of experiences.

Journey

How can I be in beginner's mind right now?

–2–

Direct Revelation

I consider it to be our birthright
to practice direct revelation and to be in contact
with our personal spiritual guidance.

—SANDRA INGERMAN

Shamanism is, first and foremost, a practice of direct revelation. Your experience of shamanism is about your own connection to the sacred, to your own sources of spiritual assistance. Although some religions define this as claiming communication from God, we are using direct revelation to simply mean your own experience with the sacred. While human teachers can help guide you based on their experience and traditions, shamanism is not about blindly following anyone or any rigid set of practices. What is your current relationship to the sacred around you? To the sacred within you? Perhaps you're in frequent dialogue with helping spirits through a traditional shamanic journeying practice. Perhaps you are just beginning to explore your own spirituality. Wherever you are, let's ask for guidance about direct revelation today.

Journey

How can I best prepare myself to hear (feel, see, and know) information from my helping spirits?

Power Animal

In the beginning of all things,
wisdom and knowledge were with the animals.

—CHIEF LETAKOS-LESA

One of the classic ways to work is in partnership with an animal spirit who is willing to help you. Journeys to meet animal spirits often begin in the Lower World.

You may already have a power animal or animal spirit with whom you connect. If so, go and visit with that animal today and spend some quality time. If not, journey to the Lower World* and ask to be shown a compassionate animal spirit who is willing to help you, perhaps with guidance, protection, companionship, and by sharing its power with you.

Journey

Journey to an animal spirit and simply spend time together. Today, whether meeting a spirit you know or someone new, just notice what (and how) they communicate with you, and what you experience together in the Lower World.

---

* If you haven't journeyed before, please see the "How to Journey" section at the beginning of this book. This is important before asking questions of helping spirits in a shamanic setting.

Drumming

Drum sound rises on the air, its throb, my heart.
A voice inside the beat says, "I know you're tired, but come.
This is the way."

—RUMI

Percussion is a foundation of shamanic practice. It shifts us out of our ordinary state of consciousness into a place where we can experience new dimensions of spiritual awareness and support. We have a primal connection to a drumbeat, beginning perhaps with hearing the rhythm of our mother's heartbeat while in the womb. From a very early age, kids often make drums out of found objects, like pots and tabletops. As adults, we can still use objects at hand; a pack of Tic Tac® mints is an effective impromptu rattle, for example. Use what you have, purchase or make a new instrument, or use a recorded shamanic drumming track to aid you in your journeys. There is a recording available from my website, WholeSpirit.com.

Journey

The focus of today's journey is the drumming itself. If you have a drum, play it with a consistent, steady beat. If you don't have a drum, listen to a recording of some shamanic drumming. Simply let your body soak in the vibration of the drum. Pay attention to how you feel before, during, and after.

"Seeing" Like a Shaman

*What you see with your eyes shut
is what counts.*

—JOHN LAME DEER

Although the word *shaman* derives from the Tungus language, many cultures have a word for a person who plays a similar role. One frequent similarity of those words cross-culturally is that they describe the shaman's ability to "see" in unusual ways and with heightened senses. "Seeing with shaman's eyes" involves more than the physical senses. In fact, shamans are said to be able to see in the dark. The Matsigenka Indians of the Upper Amazon call a shaman "one who sees." The Hmong shamans of Southeast Asia call it "seeing with the heart." Shamans use many kinds of sensing to experience the spiritual dimensions, connect with helping spirits, gather information, and perform healings. You don't have to be a shaman to explore the use of expanded sensing to perceive the world around you.

Journey

Please show me how to see with "shaman's eyes."

Web of Connection

If all the beasts were gone, men would die
from a great loneliness of spirit,
for whatever happens to the beasts
also happens to the man.
All things are connected.
Whatever befalls the Earth
befalls the sons of the Earth.

—CHIEF SEATTLE

The universal web of light and life is a concept familiar to many religious traditions, from Native Americans to the Unitarian Universalists. We are all connected. Everything that is alive affects everything else to varying degrees. How are you both affected by and affecting this web? Can you be more conscious in this relationship?

Journey

How can I be more conscious in my relationship to the web of light and life?

Balance: Upright in Upheaval

Both the making and the unmaking
were essential parts of life
and necessary to keep the balance.

—WINONA LADUKE

One of the basic principles of shamanic practice is seeking balance by creating it actively, with our thoughts, words, deeds, and actions. Cultivating a balanced life is easier during some times than others.

At times it feels like the ground under our feet is moving. What once felt solid begins to move in unpredictable and disorienting ways. We expect this on the ocean, but not on dry land. One option is to collapse to the ground and hang on until the upheaval is over; however, this is not necessarily the most productive response. We can develop "sea legs" that help us recalibrate to an environment in frequent motion.

What tools can you use to keep your balance—while staying upright—when times feel really shaky? Let's ask.

Journey

Journey for guidance about keeping balanced during times of upheaval.

Heartstorming

*The greatest distance in the world
is the 14 inches from our minds
to our hearts.*

—GRANDMOTHER AGNES BAKER PILGRIM

The term "brainstorming" is common—throwing out a lot of ideas to solve a problem without judging them as they come. Brainstorming is a great technique to gather a lot of ideas quickly and avoid the stifling inertia that comes when we start analyzing and doubting ourselves immediately. As the term implies, brainstorming is focused on the brain, on our mental processing, what we *think*.

What if we practiced "heartstorming" instead? What if we intentionally connected with our hearts and then followed the same process as brainstorming, allowing a free flow of ideas, those that come from what we *feel*? This can be done alone or in groups, and results in a heart-centered way of gathering ideas and information, helping us understand our deepest desires and motivations.

Journey

Heartstorm about something you've been working on. Ask your helping spirits to join and support you as you make a list of ideas—no editing, judging, or belittling. After you have the list, pare it down to the ones that really inspire and have meaning for you.

Spirit Teacher

Those who know do.
Those that understand, teach.

—ARISTOTLE

We've journeyed to the Lower World to meet an animal spirit. Today, go to the Upper World* and seek out a spirit teacher, strengthening your network and building your personal pantheon. If you are already working with a spirit teacher, visit with them today and spend some quality time. If you aren't, journey to the Upper World and ask to be shown a compassionate helping spirit who is willing to help you, perhaps with guidance, protection, companionship, and by sharing their power with you. As with all good teachers, spirit teachers are there to inspire and illuminate.

Journey

Journey to a spirit teacher and simply spend time together. Today, whether meeting a spirit you know or someone new, pay attention to what (and how) they communicate with you, and what you experience together in the Upper World.

---

* If you haven't journeyed to the Upper World before, please see the "How to Journey" section at the beginning of this book.

Experience Your Body

*I acknowledge the privilege of being alive
in a human body at this moment,
endowed with senses, memories, emotions, thoughts,
and the space of mind in its wisdom aspect.*

—ALEX GREY

Today is about simply feeling your body. As usual, you can do this in journey form, or as a meditation. Focus your attention and intention on fully awakening to the sensations and wisdom of your physical body.

Journey

Bring your attention to your feet and feel your toes. Slowly, mindfully, move to your ankles, then calves. Gradually work your way up to the top of your head. Feel your skin and the parts of your body that are external and touch the air. Connect with the organs that are internal and self-contained. Be present and quiet. By listening, you can also hear if there is information for you today.

The Next Normal

When you do not take your interactions so personally,
you will be able to see that each offers you
a choice—to see yourself as a victim
who reacts to the circumstances of your life,
or as a creator who chooses your responses to them.

—GARY ZUKAV

Change usually happens incrementally and subtly. We don't realize the full effect of the constant state of change we're in until we get a little distance. However, there are times when life changes suddenly. These periods bring change of such magnitude that we mark time by them—before and after. Sometimes these are personal events that alter life's trajectory, like the birth of a child or the death of a beloved spouse. Sometimes they are collective experiences, like a pandemic or war. In either instance, life as we'd known it shifts and doesn't look quite the same way after the event. We need to adjust to the new world we find ourselves in, hopefully adapting and evolving in the process.

Journey

Journey to ask for guidance about adjusting to life after a momentous event. How can you make the most of your "next normal?"

Underwater

Reality whistles a different tune underwater.

—Tom Robbins

When we see from perspectives outside our usual vantage point, we expand our abilities to observe and interact with the world. Traveling throughout the country, throughout the world, has this effect, and it helps us learn something about ourselves in the process. Today, we move into a different world to see through new eyes and feel with new senses.

We are exploring the extraordinary realms that exist underwater. An incredible variety of creatures live in the oceans and seas; some are familiar and some are astonishing and alien to us. What would it be like to live underwater? How would our perspective of the nature of reality change? Is there anything about a temporary experience of that vantage point that might help you live your life above water with a little more insight, understanding, and depth?

Journey

Ask one of your helping spirits to take you underwater to experience the world from a sea creature's point of view.

Signs in Nature

A sense of wild is engendered by awareness,
a sense of connection with and deep understanding
of any landscape. The pavement of any city side street
wriggles with enough life to terrify
and delight us if we choose
to immerse ourselves in it.

—Tristan Gooley

Nature holds a wealth of information for us—practical literal information about staying in equilibrium, but also personal information. Part of seeing with shaman's eyes is to become attuned to the elements, animals, and plants, both in their interactions with each other and in their interactions with us. By becoming attuned like this, we can develop the ability to interpret the signs in nature and are often provided with valuable guidance for living healthier, happier lives.

Journey

Think of a question. Pay close attention to the world around you today—especially, but not only, the natural world. Consider what you witness and experience in relation to your question.

Air

Some old-fashioned things
like fresh air and sunshine
are hard to beat.

—LAURA INGALLS WILDER

The element of air surrounds us and sustains us. We cannot live without it, even for a few moments. Despite our dependence on air, it is the least tangible of the elements. It takes many forms, each with a different lesson for us. At times it's gentle and still (a dawn meadow in spring); at other times it's violent and fast (a tornado or hurricane). Sometimes it's sweet and intimate (the breath of a sleeping child on your shoulder); other times it's sour and impersonal (a busy city street filled with cars, buses, and taxis at rush hour). What does the spirit of air hold for you today?

Journey

Journey to the spirit of air and see what air has to show you today.

Something New

*Each time you learn something new
you readjust the whole framework
of your knowledge.*

—ELEANOR ROOSEVELT

Routines can be reassuring, allowing us to find our natural rhythms. When a routine begins to feel less comforting and more numbing, it's time to mix things up. Have you ever felt bored or antsy and just wanted to try something new? Maybe you had an idea of what that thing was. Maybe you had no idea, but craved the excitement that new experiences can bring. Let's seek that today in non-ordinary reality.

Journey

Journey to a power animal or spirit teacher and ask them to help you experience something new.

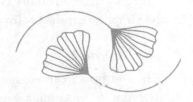

Invisible and Visible

*Invisible things
are the most powerful of all.*
—RABBI DR. SHAUL MARSHALL PRAVER

As a visual culture, we tend to ascribe power and validity to what we can see. However, many "invisible" things are incredibly powerful—love, power, greed, lust. Sometimes, we undermine our perceptions of the invisible simply because we don't have tangible evidence. Part of developing a strong spiritual sense is to recognize and give credence to what is felt as well as what is seen, to engage the invisible, energetic aspects of life as intentionally, and ethically, as we would the visible. For example, has someone ever smiled at you and said something sweet—and it felt bad? Consider the expression on someone's face and the words they speak, but pay at least as much attention to the energy they carry. Smiles and sweet words cannot truly hide a mean spirit. We're responsible for our own thoughts and intentions as well as our outward expressions; others will sense the whole of who we are. The energy we embody impacts our relationships and has concrete implications in our lives.

Journey

Please help me understand how I can engage the invisible realms more effectively by understanding where the invisible is affecting the visible in my life.

Open Guidance

*No matter who we are
or where we live,
thanks to the nearly ageless presence
of shamanism in the world
we each have ancestral ties
to one or more
of the world's shamanic traditions.*

—NAN MOSS

Asking specific questions creates a clear intention and is powerful. Today, we balance structure and flow by leaving our question open.

Journey

What do I need to know today?

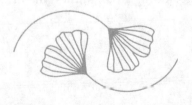

Vulnerability

When we were children,
we used to think that
when we were grown up
we would no longer be vulnerable.
But to grow up
is to accept vulnerability. . . .
To be alive is to be vulnerable.

—MADELEINE L'ENGLE

Our ideas and opinions often feel like precious things. Expressing them can leave us feeling exposed and vulnerable. We can be deeply affected by the responses we get from others, both the positive and negative. Today, ask for healing around any wounds that occurred when you shared your feelings or ideas and they were not received as you would have liked.

Journey

Please give me healing around times when I was vulnerable and hurt.

Energy Focus

Successful people
maintain a positive focus in life
no matter what is going on around them.

—JACK CANFIELD

The word *focus* comes from the Latin "hearth" or "fire-place." The hearth was traditionally the center of power of the home, radiating warmth and sustenance. Where is your focus, your center of power? We can change what we focus on depending on our goals and intentions, and our focus can become more diffuse or intense.

Periodically, it's good to think about how (and where) we want to focus, or refocus, our resources. Time, money, emotional investments, work efforts, and social interactions are all areas that are worth reviewing from time to time to see if the energy we are devoting to them aligns with our priorities and goals.

Journey

Where should I focus my energy right now?

Spirit in Everything

We live immersed in a sea of energy
beyond all comprehension.
But this energy, in an ultimate sense,
is ours not by domination
but by invocation.

—Thomas Berry

Categorizing and differentiating sometimes make it easier to organize and comprehend the world around us. But the process of labeling can also reduce and limit our understanding of things that are more complicated or nuanced. For example, sometimes we talk about spirit being one place or another. We go to temples, churches, mosques and other "sacred" places to connect with the divine. Yet spirit is everywhere, perhaps no more in those places than in a forest, a classroom, or on a bustling street. When we recognize the spirit in everything and everyone, we move away from differentiation and into integration and interconnectedness. We start to acknowledge the ways everything affects and is affected by everything else. Everything is sacred.

Journey

Ask a helping spirit to help you see spirit in everything.

Heaven on Earth

Without stirring abroad,
One can know the whole world;
Without looking out of the window
One can see the way of heaven.
The further one goes
The less one knows.

—LAO TZU

What is your ideal place to be? Today, let's envision a place that feels heavenly to you. Mine may be a balmy natural retreat with a pool and waterfall, emerald-green moss, fig trees, lush vegetation and fragrant flowers tumbling over ancient rock walls. Throw in some goats and kittens milling around, fresh fruit and . . . Okay, I got lost there for a moment. That's actually the point. Experience an environment that is so lovely to you that you slip into it and are in heaven for a little while.

Engage all your senses—see it, smell it, hear it, taste it. What does this place *feel* like? Are you there alone or with others? What emotions does it inspire in you?

Journey

Journey to experience your heaven on Earth.

Answers

To be truly visionary
we have to root our imagination
in our concrete reality
while simultaneously imagining possibilities
beyond that reality.

—BELL HOOKS

Do you have a question (issue, problem, dilemma) that you've been mulling over for a while with seemingly no progress toward an answer? Today is the day to address it. Try to clear your mind of your past deliberations. Turn this question over to your helping spirits.

As you journey, try to be as open and receptive as possible to whatever you are shown, whatever you hear, whatever sensations you have in your body. When you return, write, record, draw, or in some way document it as thoroughly as possible *without* trying to come to a conclusion. Let it sit a while. Then come back and review and see what insights you have about your questions.

Journey

What is the answer to my question?

Community

Until recently,
in every part of the world
communities of indigenous peoples
functioned as if one
with their particular environment.

—CAROL SCHAEFER

We use the word "community" frequently in different contexts. How do you define community? How do you create community? How do you take part in one? Whether small or large, intentional or more haphazard, we are all part of multiple communities. Let's ask for guidance about being more conscious about how we create, engage, and affect the communities we are a part of or wish we had in our lives.

Journey

Please give me guidance about my role in the communities in my life (and the role these communities play in my life).

Directions

Every man has to learn
the points of the compass again
as often as he awakes,
whether from sleep or any abstraction.

—Henry David Thoreau

For many of us, navigating is as simple as entering an address into the maps program of our phone or into a GPS. When was the last time you used a paper map? Have you ever? Imagine a time before paper maps existed, or when there were only a few precious master copies.

Not all that long ago, most people got around based on their own knowledge of the landscape, and how the world was oriented. If I said to you, "Go south!" would you be able to follow that direction at any time of day or night? Perhaps now would be a good time to rekindle your relationship with the directions. Reorienting ourselves to north, south, east, and west in the physical world is a complementary practice to honoring the spirit of those directions.

Journey

Journey to ask how you can create a better relationship to the directions.

Gifts for the Earth

Power is in the earth;
it is in your relationship
to the earth.

—WINONA LADUKE

We depend on the Earth and her resources for just about everything. We are so accustomed to this that it's easy to take it for granted. However, people are becoming increasingly aware of the depletion of the Earth's resources and how urgent it is that we come into balance in our relationship with her. Yet even when we want to do something kind in return, we may not always know what is really useful, and might make assumptions that aren't accurate.

Journey

Journey to the spirit of the Earth and ask for guidance about what the Earth would like to receive from us.

Radiant Love

Darkness cannot drive out darkness;
only light can do that.
Hate cannot drive out hate;
only love can do that.

—DR. MARTIN LUTHER KING JR.

Research is backing up the instinctual belief that love is an agent for positive change. A sampling of the studies on loving-kindness meditation yield the following benefits: increased joy, contentment, hope, gratitude, relaxation, amusement, and awe, and decreased anger, depression, and PTSD.

Journey

For today's journey, think about where you want to direct a loving intention. It can be to a person, animal, community, place, or cause. You are not trying to do healing work without permission. You are simply letting yourself be filled with the energy of love and allowing that to radiate. If this feels challenging, start with something easy. For example, if you love your dog absurdly, as I do, think of her. Focus on your feelings of love for her, and you will naturally enter a loving state. Then let that loving energy flow freely in the direction you choose.

Inner Wisdom

This is inner knowledge, or gnosis—
the certainty that people feel
when they respond to deep recognition
or know the significance
of the choice they are making,
while not knowing where it will lead
and that others are likely to not understand.
—JEAN SHINODA BOLEN

Are you prone to looking outside for guidance? Looking inward is a helpful first step to cultivating wisdom. In this journey, let's honor the wisdom that you hold within and encourage it to play a more vocal and vigorous role in your life.

Journey

I honor my inner wisdom and ask that it show itself audibly and actively in my life today.

Responsibility

A sense of calm came over me.
More and more often
I found myself thinking,
"This is where I belong.
This is what I came into this world to do."

—JANE GOODALL

What are we responsible for and what can we let go of? Some of us feel the weight of the world's suffering (responsible for everything and everyone); others are impervious to suffering when it is not our own (responsible for little). Most of us fall somewhere in the middle. Let's ask for guidance about our own relationship to responsibility. Are we attending to what and to whom we should? Are we balanced in our levels of empathy to others and attention to ourselves? Are there adjustments to be made?

Journey

Journey to ask for guidance about how you are handling responsibility in your life.

Shadow and Light

*Shamanism is the ability to light up
what others perceive as darkness.*

—Michael Harner

There is no need to fear the dark. No one is all light. Dark and light are sides of a coin, part of a whole. Dark is natural, not negative. The nighttime is a place of beauty. It helps us to sleep and rejuvenate, and it is a quiet time when nocturnal animals roam. But what is in shadow is concealed, and sometimes what is hidden needs to be illuminated in order for healing and awareness to take place. Bringing light is honoring the natural cycle of illumination, as day follows night, waking follows sleeping, and blooming aboveground follows roots growing below. If we develop a fear of the dark, we stunt our development, denying natural parts of ourselves, and giving power to the hidden. It's healing to seek out and work with what needs to be illuminated.

Journey

What is in the shadows right now that is ready to come into the light?

Inclusivity

Peace requires everyone to be in the circle—
wholeness, inclusion.

—ISABEL ALLENDE

We each have our own identity, background, and opinions that shape how we experience the world. These differences are a beautiful part of being human, but it's hard to live peacefully with one another when we either exclude or feel excluded because of these differences. Part of our inner spiritual work is shining light on areas where we may inadvertently hold beliefs that are exclusionary, biased, or prejudiced. It can be upsetting to find these qualities within ourselves, but if we don't search unflinchingly for these beliefs, they can affect our actions and how we engage in our communities. Exclusions can happen by default if we don't take action toward inclusion.

Journey

Please show me if there are areas where I could be more inclusive in my thoughts, attitudes, and actions.

What Does My Body Need?

The body knows things
a long time before the mind catches up to them.
I was wondering what my body knew
that I didn't.

—SUE MONK KIDD

From the shamanic perspective, the energy or spirit of our bodies provides the foundation for our health. When we take on what isn't ours, become dispirited, or disconnect from our power, those imbalances can ripple outward and cause physical issues.

With busy lives, it's easy to get disconnected from what our bodies are communicating to us. Subtle clues are often overlooked until more obvious signs like pain and illness emerge. Listening to your physical self on a regular basis gives you valuable information about what your body needs to be healthy.

Journey

What does my body need today?

Play

*Hindus, when they speak of
the creation of the universe,
do not call it the work of God;
they call it the play of God.*

—ALAN WATTS

How do you play? Now think of your parent, or your child, or one of your coworkers—do they have fun playing in the same way? What is fun for one person is not necessarily fun for another. Finding what is genuinely "play" for you is important. We can hold some stereotypical ideas about what is supposed to be fun and playful (parties, sports, board games), when in reality those things may be the antithesis of fun for you. A balanced life includes work and play, seriousness and lightheartedness. It's important to explore where you can genuinely find the energy of play that suits you.

Journey

Create some open space in your life for play today. If you need guidance around this, ask for help.

Adapting to Time and Place

In the long history of humankind
(and animal kind, too) those who learned
to collaborate and improvise most effectively
have prevailed.

—CHARLES DARWIN

Shamanism has survived for tens of thousands of years in large part because it adapts to the time and place in which it exists. One place and time is not more "authentic" than any other. It is important to align our practices with the times and places we are in. Imitating cultures of old in a rigid way will not produce results for us today. We need to source power from here and now.

The enduring power of shamanism provides a good model for us in every aspect of life. We grow, evolve, and thrive when we retain our authenticity and identity as we adapt to changing situations.

Journey

Are there ways that I need to change to better align with this time and place in order to grow and evolve?

Roots and Branches

*Deep roots are not reached
by the frost.*

—J. R. R. TOLKIEN

If I asked you, "Where are your roots?" what would you think about? Maybe genealogy, gardening, cultural history, or spirituality? Or maybe where you store your supply of ginger or turmeric? But I'm talking about something else. I'm talking about what you are grounded in—your beliefs, your convictions, your identity. Having strong roots helps us weather storms and grow strong and healthy branches, perhaps yielding fruit or flowers. Ask for guidance about how to strengthen your roots today. It may be in one particular area, or in your life as a whole. You can choose where to focus or leave it up to your helping spirits.

Journey

How can I strengthen my roots to grow stronger branches?

Be Kind, Live Longer

I want to be a fire-breathing dragon.
Except I will be a flower-breathing dragon.
I will blow flowers all over the house
and I will be nice.

—VIOLET, AGE 4

Being kind and caring may actually help you live longer. A University of Michigan study has shown that people who are "helpful to others reduce their risk of dying by nearly 60 percent." Let's try to perform a few random acts of kindness today. Either let them come spontaneously, or ask your helping spirits for guidance about where your kindness is most needed.

Journey

Be especially kind and caring to others today. Ask for guidance if you like.

Humility

I hold tight to the vision
that some day soon we will find
the courage of self-restraint,
the humility to live like mosses.

—Robin Wall Kimmerer

What does it mean to be right-sized? There is a subtle and elusive sweet spot when it comes to humility. Too much and you are not honoring yourself, too little and you can edge into pride or boastfulness, too much overt discussion about it and it feels inauthentic. Only you can really know how you want to show up in the world. Helping spirits can be brutally honest, extremely kind, and absurdly funny. They tell us things about ourselves that we wouldn't accept from another human being. Let's check in with our helping spirits today about our egos and their relative size. Do you need some bolstering, or might you need a reality check about yourself?

Journey

Spirits, please show me if I need some adjustment around my ego.

Quality Time

Here in the journeying domain
I found a sense of calm, softness,
protection, and devotion.
My experience of the animal's
commitment to my welfare
strengthened with each encounter.

—JEANNETTE M. GAGAN

Nurturing healthy relationships, in ordinary and non-ordinary reality, involves being together, conversing, and exploring, not just asking for something. As with ordinary reality relationships, our relationships with helping spirits benefit from quality one-on-one time.

Journey

Journey to a helping spirit of your choice and simply spend time together.

Honoring Our Tools

We become what we behold.
We shape our tools
and then our tools shape us.

—MARSHALL McLUHAN

If you own a drum or a rattle, today is a day to honor it. When we relate to our tools as purely inanimate objects, we miss an opportunity to really care for them. Shamans honor their tools. Mongolian shamans historically used liquor distilled from mare's milk, or more commonly today, vodka, to honor and cleanse their drums and other ceremonial objects. "Spirits for the spirits." If you don't own a drum or rattle, that's okay; honor another tool that you use regularly.

Journey

If you have a drum (or rattle), give it some extra love today. Perhaps play it and journey to honor it. If you don't have a drum, pick something else that contributes to the quality of your life and say thank you.

The Elements Within You

*Our individual composition
is the same as the composition
of the rest of the universe.*

—AYYA KHEMA

We contain all the elements within us, literally and arche-typally. Do you know anyone with a fiery personality? How about an earth mother? Stereotypes oversimplify our ener-getic personalities and the nature of the elements them-selves, but understanding how we embody the elements gives us valuable information for balancing our selves and our relationships. As in the natural world, all elements are present to varying degrees within us. The health of our internal ecosystem is affected by whether that mixture is harmonious or out of whack. For example, a person with a lot of water in their energetic archetype can be adapt-able, intuitive, creative, and persevering. Too much water and there can be inflammation, stagnation, and emotional imbalance. In that case, it might be helpful to add one or more of the other three elements. Have a fire ceremony, a day outside in the wind, or some grounding to bring the solidity of earth into the mix. Let's ask your helping spirits for information about your elemental energy personality.

Journey

Please show me anything I need to see about my relation to the archetypal elements within me.

Authenticity

There are people who practice authenticity
and people who don't.
The people who practice authenticity
work their ass off at it.

—BRENÉ BROWN

Have you ever been in a situation where you didn't feel comfortable being yourself? Maybe you acted a part to fit in or felt you might be judged if you showed your true self. Did it make you a little queasy? We don't have to share our innermost selves all the time to be authentic, but when we speak or act in ways that are not congruent with our beliefs, or who we truly are, we create a spiritual dissonance. This has internal effects on our well-being, and it can be sensed by others around us. At times we can be unaware that we are out of congruence. Fear, ambition, desire, and many other strong emotions can pull us a bit off course. Let's check in today and see if there are any areas where authenticity needs to be reassessed.

Journey

Are there any areas in my life where I am not being truly authentic, and if so, what can I do to change them?

What Needs Seeing?

Maybe life doesn't get any better than this,
or any worse,
and what we get
is just what we're willing to find:
small wonders, where they grow.

—Barbara Kingsolver

Sometimes we don't know the most relevant questions to ask. Our perspectives are naturally limited, and so our requests can be, too. It is sometimes important to ask to be shown what needs to be seen. The helping spirits may be able to help us best by illuminating what is beyond our current vantage point.

Journey

Please show me what needs to be seen.

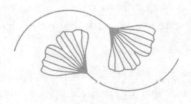

Power of the Invisible:
Sparking Change

What we achieve inwardly
will change outer reality.

—PLUTARCH

All the great traditions, including shamanism, assert that change comes from within, from the invisible realms. In shamanism there is direct engagement with the spirit that animates and connects us all. In the Vedic tradition, this force is called *prana*. In many Eastern traditions it is *ch'i or ki*. In the Pacific region it is *mana*. The Jewish mystical theosophy of Kabbalah refers to it as astral light. Whatever we call it, it is a potent source for changing the visible world, including the health of our bodies, the quality of our relationships, and the circumstances of our lives. The ancient tenet "As within so without, as above so below" illustrates the interrelationship between inner and outer, visible and invisible that is so important in shamanic philosophy. Change starts from within. Is there anything you would like to change in outer reality? Ask for guidance today about what changes in your internal state would spark that outer change.

Journey

Please show me what internal changes I can make to help change _____ in the external world.

Honoring Elders

*Children need the wisdom of their elders;
the aging need the encouragement
of a child's exuberance.*

—CORRIE TEN BOOM

It's hard to align a respect for age and wisdom with our cultural obsession with the smoothness of youth. This fixation on youthful beauty contributes to a devaluing of the elders. If we shun the appearance of age, rejecting it, fearing it and hiding it, we are by extension shunning (rejecting, fearing, hiding) people of certain ages. Wisdom often comes with time. Yes, our youth have much to contribute and much to teach, but we should respect the wisdom our elders can offer, too. Especially in these times of radical speed in technological advancement, it becomes easy to feel that we are worlds apart, communicating in different ways, but it's important that we find a common language so that we can benefit from the experience of those who have come before us.

Journey

How can I be in right relationships with my elders?

Pronoia

*The universe is conspiring
to shower you with blessings.*

—ROB BREZSNY

What we believe dramatically impacts what we experience. Rob Brezsny describes *pronoia* as the belief that "the universe is conspiring to shower you with blessings." This is quite different from how many people perceive reality. When we view the world through the lens of suspicion, our beliefs are usually realized. When we treat others suspiciously, they begin to treat us in kind, communications go awry, relationships sour, we wind up lonely, and our original supposition is confirmed—the world is out to get us. What if we flipped that and practiced pronoia as Brezsny suggests? Not a Pollyanna approach, with everything artificially tinted rose, but with the attitude that everything can be nourishing, that life, however wrenching or tragic, is somehow as it should be. Fundamentally, the universe is rooting for us. Whether or not it's true, practice it for a while and see what it feels like.

Journey

In today's journey, go to whichever world you like, and imagine all your helping spirits conspiring to help you. Observe what that feels like. If you choose, commit to spending time each day in a state of pronoia.

States of Consciousness

When I was to be a shaman,
I chose suffering through the two things
that are most dangerous to us humans,
suffering through hunger
and suffering through cold.

—Igjugârjuk

In shamanic practice, percussion is often used to shift into an altered state of consciousness. Practitioners sometimes use psychedelic plants to guide them. Fasting and deprivation are classic ways to change states. Dancing moves us, like the Sufis whirling into ecstasy and the ceremonial dances of powwows, as can singing, making art, intense states of love, or sex. Dreaming is an altered state we enter into every night. There are many ways to shift states. Depending on the person, the intention, and the situation, we have ample opportunities to expand our capacity for spiritual perception, insight, and relationship.

Journey

In today's journey, use one of these methods to shift your state, to move from thinking mode to experiential mode. Set a clear intention before starting that you are safe in your space, ask your helping spirits to be with you, and give yourself ample time to come back from your experience and into your regular state of consciousness.

Creativity and Imagination

*You can't depend on your eyes
when your imagination is out of focus.*

—Mark Twain

In childhood, specific times are often devoted to creativity and imagination. We did arts and crafts and pretend games, we read fantastic stories with wacky characters and rich illustrations, and we sang songs or learned to play instruments. As we get older, creativity is often set aside for jobs and responsibilities. Today, let's ask for help in identifying how we can bring creativity into our lives in ways that are joyful, inspiring, and fun.

Journey

Journey to ask for help in bringing creativity into your life today.

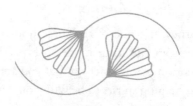

Heartbreak

If you're really listening,
if you're awake to the poignant beauty of the world,
your heart breaks regularly.
In fact, your heart is made to break;
its purpose is to burst open again and again
so it can hold evermore wonders.

—ANDREW HARVEY

Any spiritual path, including shamanism, will help moor us during times of intensity. We all come into this world tenderhearted. Over time we develop different ways of reacting when our hearts feel bruised or broken. When we have an absence of spiritual connection, those times of feeling broken can be unbearable. Actually, those times can *always* feel unbearable, yet when we've established a spiritual mooring, we're better able to find the end of the rope and pull ourselves back onto shore. When we evolve spiritually we're able to feel both suffering and joy more intensely, and possibly take them less personally. When we don't shut down, each bruising can be a chance to mend stronger, to expand our capacity to feel, as Andrew Harvey says, to "hold evermore wonders."

Journey

Please show me something wondrous that has come from heartbreak in my life.

Loving Yourself

For small creatures such as we
the vastness is bearable only through love.

—Carl Sagan

Most of us have things that we find unlovable about ourselves. It may be something physical or a part of our personality, and when we think about it, we definitely do not love it. It's something we go out of our way to change or hide. Let's send love to that part of ourselves today.

Journey

Send love to a part of yourself that you find hard to love.

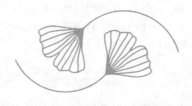

Rocks

We have forgotten
what rocks and plants still know
—we have forgotten how to be
—to be still
—to be ourselves
—to be where life is here and now.

—ECKHART TOLLE

Rocks are the bones of the Earth. Deep down, they move and shift and also provide stability, not unlike the way our skeletons do. Like other beings of nature, rocks can impart wisdom to us if we take time to connect with them. Whether they are river rocks worn smooth by water, jagged boulders supporting a mountainside, red rock canyons, or little stones along a path in the woods, pay attention to the rocks you encounter today. And for our journey, let's listen to what the rocks have to say.

Journey

Ask your helping spirits to take you to a rock that is willing to connect with you. Be with it and see what it has to communicate. Notice with all your senses, remembering that different beings have different ways to communicate.

The Void

If you look long enough into the void,
the void begins to look back through you.

—Friedrich Nietzsche

I love NASA's amazing photos of space taken from the Hubble Space Telescope. The Swan Nebula is particularly gorgeous. Many of us have a conception of space as being vast blackness. These photos tell a different story. Everything starts from the void. Everything that comes into being has a backstory in pure potential. That place of potential is the void. Because the many possibilities it holds are not yet visible, we find this place mysterious and maybe a little frightening. However, when we learn to work with it, we find extraordinary power. How can you seed the void with the highest possibilities for your life and the life of all beings? Like providing a seed with all the best nutrients, how might you change (and be changed by) what happens in this space of raw creative power? Focus less on a specific vision and more on the energy you wish to see manifested. For example, if you are looking for a life partner, maybe focus less on the specifics of how you want that person to look and more on how you'll be inspired by authentic partnership.

Journey

Ask your helping spirits to take you to the void and plant your highest creative intention there.

Sexuality

Except in the modern world,
sexuality everywhere and always
has been a hierophany.

—Mircea Eliade

Bring your spirit to bed. Sexuality is a powerful way to express spirituality. Many of us have sexual wounds. Since the images about sex that pervade our culture are often twisted and disconnected from spirit, it's easy to feel that those aspects of ourselves need to be kept separate. Sexuality is complicated, and it's also a tremendous opportunity for healing. When we have sex, we unite with others in the most intimate and vulnerable ways. What would sex be like if we were always attuned to our highest spiritual selves as we connected physically with our bodies? Are there areas of healing that may be needed for you to feel safe in this area? Or is this one of the places where you can really be you, free, connected, and able to express yourself in deep and meaningful ways?

Journey

Is there anything about my sexuality I should be aware of right now, for my highest good and for those with whom I am intimate?

Mushrooming Networks

Mycelium is Earth's natural internet.

—Paul Stamets

Mushrooms, the fruit of mycelial networks, have an incredibly diverse and long history of healing applications. Their communication webs can be vast—check out the humongous fungus of Oregon. They also have amazing powers of collaboration. The symbiotic relationships between fungi and plants, called mycorrhiza, send data and nutrients back and forth. A whopping 90 percent of plants depend on these reciprocal relationships for robust health. We are often conditioned to think in terms of competition, but in nature, there are cooperative underpinnings to the operating system. What if we began looking at each other in the same way, cooperatively rather than competitively?

Journey

How can I shift to a cooperative rather than competitive mindset for the increased well-being of myself and others?

Lion

I can also change into a lion.
When I go into the bush,
I make this change.
As a lion, I dance with people
in the healing dance.

—Ngwaga Osele

From sculptures of the lion-headed Egyptian deity Sekmet, to the cave paintings of Lascaux in France, to carvings from ancient Mesopotamia of the goddess Inanna standing atop them, lions have played a prominent role cross-culturally. They are regal, used to symbolize protection, and unfortunately hunted as trophies. What might we learn from a relationship with lion? How might a lion teach us differently from a lioness?

Journey

Journey to a lion or lioness and ask if there is something he or she is willing to teach you.

What's Missing?

And in general,
the residents of the town wondered
why they all felt hollow
just beneath the throat,
the result of missing something
they had never been able to name
in the first place.

—JODI PICOULT

Is there something missing in your life right now? Are there steps you could take to address that absence? Let's leave this question wide open for guidance. You may know exactly what this is (have you been fixating on it?) or you may be surprised by what comes up. This could be a seemingly small detail of physical life like a vitamin or book to read, or it could be a macro-level energy like patience, for example.

Journey

Is there something that I'm missing? If so, please show me how to address it.

Wise Power

The most common way
people give up their power
is by thinking they don't have any.

—ALICE WALKER

When you think of power, what comes to mind? Physical strength, social influence, political clout, brainpower? Power is fascinating and complex, with very real implications in our personal and collective lives. Shamanic paths talk about power, and it's important to be clear on what that means. When one develops an aspect of their being they can be more powerful, and with that increased power comes the need for more responsibility. For example, if you work out and get stronger muscles, you have more power to harm another being. It is incumbent on you to use that physical strength wisely. If you cultivate knowledge and learn the workings of the law, it is incumbent on you to use your knowledge ethically. The same is true of spiritual power. As you increase your spiritual power, you may find you have new insights or other abilities that you'll need to navigate. Power is neutral. It's fuel. We decide what we're going to create with increased power of any kind.

Journey

Spirits, please guide me in the wise and ethical use of my spiritual power.

Perfection

In this broad earth of ours,
Amid the measureless grossness and the slag,
Enclosed and safe within its central heart,
Nestles the seed perfection.

—WALT WHITMAN

Do you walk around feeling perfect? Probably not. As human beings we generally have lost sight of the experience of our spiritual wholeness. There are many things keeping us separate from that feeling of divine perfection: the aches and pains of our bodies, the insecurities and worries of our minds, all the basic experiences of having an ego. But we are more than our bodies, minds, and past experiences, and when you shift your attention away from them, you experience what you are at your core: spiritual light. Perfect.

Journey

As you journey today, ask a helping spirit to assist you in dropping anything that keeps you from experiencing your divine perfection. Or just stay put, exactly where you are, and experience your light.

I Wish or I Am

Don't fake it till you make it.
Fake it till you become it.

—AMY CUDDY

There are different approaches to working with spiritual intentions, both in shamanic traditions and in other practices. One is asking, wishing, even begging, for what we want. When we journey and ask a helping spirit for something, we are petitioning them. We are humbly appealing to a higher source. We do this in prayer as well. We are hoping they will say yes and grant our request.

Another approach is to act as if the thing we want is already here, to state it as fact, and be grateful. This is a decree. It is active and present focused. It creates a very different energetic relationship. Feel the difference:

Please make me healthy and happy. (petition)

I am healthy and happy. Thank you. (decree)

Journey

Create your own decree, journey to one of your helping spirits, and state it with gratitude.

Crow

Like most people,
I have crow stories to tell.

—CANDACE SAVAGE

The crows know. Incredibly smart, they remember our faces, distinguishing friend from foe. Several years ago I convinced a murder (yes, a group of crows is a "murder") that I was a friend. They often came down into the yard when I whistled. I thought this was marvelous, and I loved having them so near. Sometimes they walked back and forth in front of my office window, peering in and cawing. Ultimately, I wound up going out to feed them when *they* called *me*!

Crows appear in many different mythologies, ascribed with various qualities, but always intelligence. In the Norse pantheon as Odin's familiars, and in American Indian traditions, such as the Chippewa and Pueblo, they are characterized as having a trickster element. Develop your own relationship with crows in ordinary or non-ordinary reality.

Journey

Journey to fly with a crow. What is the crow willing to show, teach, impart, or tell you today?

Creativity

The most regretful people on earth
are those who felt the call to creative work,
who felt their own creative power
restive and uprising,
and gave to it neither power nor time.

—MARY OLIVER

Creativity takes many forms. We're used to thinking about creativity in the context of the arts, but the potential to create is always present. Everyday tasks like cooking or gardening can be creative. Taking a fresh approach to a relationship can bring something new into being. Even rethinking your attitude is a creative process that has the potential to yield something useful and beautiful. Where do you need some extra juice to fuel your creativity today?

Journey

Please help me fuel my creativity.

Religion and Spirituality

Who we are cannot be separated
from where we're from.

—MALCOLM GLADWELL

Did you grow up with a particular religion? Are you still practicing it now? For some people their religion of origin remains a lifelong source of strength, while others reject it. As adults, we decide how to relate to our spirituality. For the most part, we can choose how and what we practice. Our religion of origin (or lack thereof) is important, though. Just as the place of our birth, our biological parents, and other significant aspects of our history affect us, our birth religions are relevant. Practicing shamanism does not preclude practicing a religion. Is there anything about your relationship to, or experiences with, your first religion that is relevant for you to be conscious of now?

Journey

Please show me what I need to see about my relationship with my birth religion.

Metamotivation

*If any organism
fails to fulfill its potentialities,
it becomes sick.*

—WILLIAM JAMES

When satisfying fundamental needs for things like food, shelter, and love takes up most of a person's energy, there usually isn't a lot left over for thinking about a higher purpose in life. Once there is confidence that those basic needs will be regularly met, some people are able to turn their attention to more advanced goals. Motivations shift and become about fulfilling our highest potentials in life. Psychologist Abraham Maslow coined the term "metamotivation" to describe this shift of life focus. People in this state of self-actualization may be seeking wholeness, truth, beauty, meaning, balance, justice, and other "meta"-level qualities. What motivates you?

Journey

Please show me what I need to see about my life motivations.

Conscious Technology

For a successful technology,
reality must take precedence
over public relations,
for Nature cannot be fooled.

—Richard P. Feynman

Technology is a magnificent tool—it can amplify our energetic reach. How we use technology can be another way of expressing ourselves spiritually in the world. It connects us to one another in a way that can mirror our energetic interconnectedness. We share emotions and experiences through the digital web as we do through the spiritual web of life.

What are you putting out into that web and what are you taking in from it? Technology is neither good nor bad. We choose *how* we use it, *when* we use it, and *how much* we use it.

Journey

Ask for guidance about your use of technology.

Your Garden Sanctuary

*A garden is a friend
you can visit any time.*

—OKAKURA KAKUZŌ

Today's journey is about envisioning a personal garden, a place of colorful abundance that overflows with lush beauty . . . or is it a sparse desert garden, monochromatic and Zenlike? I don't know, this is *your* garden! Whatever your ideal garden sanctuary is, experience it with all your senses. Feel yourself standing, sitting, or lying in the garden. What are the sights, sounds, and smells that surround you?

Journey

Journey to create your ideal garden sanctuary.

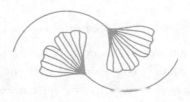

Thriving in Chaos, Step 1: Focused Observation

Accuracy of observation is the equivalent of accuracy of thinking.

—WALLACE STEVENS

If we knew what personal "weather" patterns were coming our way, we could be ready with our disaster preparation plan. We'd either brace ourselves for a quick, violent storm or settle in for a slow, brutal heat wave. But that wouldn't develop our ability to deal with the unexpected. Preparing for the possibilities, particularly in these intense and chaotic times of dissolution and reassembly, can be a significant source of stress. To create mental, physical, and emotional health, we need to stay connected to what is happening internally and externally. Then we can react appropriately, staying balanced and healthy in the face of challenging circumstances. Three steps help us thrive in chaos, intensity, and change: (1) focused observation, (2) conscious stillness, and (3) deliberate action. We'll explore them in the next three journeys.

Journey

Both in your journey and in ordinary reality today, pay close attention to what is happening around you. Watch your internal reactions to external circumstances and events. Look for patterns and themes that can help you understand what needs your attention and why.

Thriving in Chaos, Step 2: Conscious Stillness

True intelligence operates silently.
Stillness is where creativity
and solutions to problems
are found.

—ECKHART TOLLE

The second step to thriving in chaos, intensity, and change is conscious stillness. Make room for silence. Creating space for stillness with the absence of external stimuli allows your subtle senses and instincts to be heard and felt. When life gets chaotic, it's often energetically "loud." Valuable insights about how to create a healthy life can be drowned out if you don't intentionally set aside space and time to receive them.

Journey

In your journey today, be still and open, rather than actively seeking information. Creating stillness inside and out as a counterbalance for chaos helps you stay composed and ready for your next best step.

Thriving in Chaos, Step 3: Deliberate Action

You don't make progress
by standing on the sidelines,
whimpering and complaining.
You make progress
by implementing ideas.

—SHIRLEY CHISHOLM

The third step to thrive in chaos, intensity, and change is deliberate action. When the dust of the storm settles, or the lingering fog lifts, and you see a path ahead of you, step out decisively. When you sense it is time to act, do it bravely and definitively. It's easy to become paralyzed by fear, perfectionism, or having too many options. Don't worry that your action is the perfect step, just make sure that it's the next step. By blending focused observation, conscious stillness, and deliberate action, we do our part to become who we wish to be while honoring who we already are.

Journey

Ask for guidance about your next practical step.

Clear Sight

The path of illumination for the initiated
allows another vision of life,
another way of understanding
the realities of life
and one's own life.

—BERNADETTE REBIENOT

It's not possible to know the future in complete clarity. Even if we could, it probably wouldn't be beneficial. Part of the richness of life is the uncertainty of actually living it, making choices, seeing where we are led, what is surprising, and where we have opportunities to grow. However, clear sight about the here and now is helpful to get through each day in a healthy and balanced way.

Journey

Please give me clear sight to see what needs to be seen today.

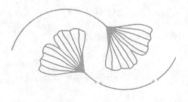

Animal Love

I think I could turn and live with the animals,
they are so placid and self contain'd;
I stand and look at them long and long.
They do not sweat and whine about their condition;
They do not lie awake in the dark and weep for their sins;
They do not make me sick discussing their duty to God;
Not one is dissatisfied—not one is demented
with the mania of owning things;
Not one kneels to another,
nor his kind that lived thousands of years ago;
Not one is responsible or industrious
over the whole earth.

—WALT WHITMAN

Few loves are purer and simpler than the love for an animal. Today, let's journey to express love for a special animal. It may be a pet (still with us or long past) or an animal from the wild (an individual or entire species).

Journey

Journey to send love to an animal.

Dream Guidance

We are so captivated by and entangled in
our subjective consciousness
that we have forgotten the age-old fact
that God speaks chiefly
through dreams and visions.

—CARL JUNG

What are your dreams trying to tell you? Are they alerting you to some upcoming event, a visitation of some sort, another way of showing you the pattern of relationships in waking life, or simply processing of the events of the day? Dream imagery is very personal. Working with your dreams can yield insight into what is happening below the surface of your everyday thoughts and activities. We dream every night whether we remember or not.

A client of mine with a vibrant dream life made a beautiful analogy when he felt he couldn't remember all his dreams. He said he felt like a bear standing in a river when the salmon are running. There were so many that he couldn't catch them all, yet any one could provide nourishment. Think of a recent dream that left an emotional resonance when you woke up, or that you found fascinating.

Journey

What is my dream trying to show me?

Art

*Art is the natural and universal language
of the human soul.*

—DAVID ELKINS

Artistic expression is enjoyable in and of itself, yet it can also help shift our internal states, allowing creativity in other aspects of life to flourish in new ways. Part of that artistic expression often engages an observer; for example, someone viewing our artwork, listening to our singing, watching our dancing, or eating our cooking. That can add some pressure.

Today, let's journey to make art in non-ordinary reality, any kind of art you want. Just enjoy it, knowing that no one is judging your talent. Focus on the experience, not the product.

Journey

Journey to make art in non-ordinary reality.

Working with Fire

*Fire that's closest kept
burns most of all.*

—William Shakespeare

Fire is a great source of transformational energy. What does heat bring to the surface for you? How does it affect the way you interact with the world? How does it "cook" and change you? Or are you fairly oblivious to it? Developing a relationship with fire can help us learn how to use the power of this element to bring healthy transformation and healing into our lives.

Journey

Journey to the spirit of fire. Introduce yourself. Ask "How can I learn from you?" If you are an experienced journeyer, consider merging with an aspect of fire with the same question. Make sure to ask permission from fire first.

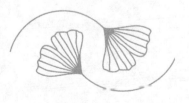

The Power of Rest

There is no music in a rest,
but there is the making of music in it.

—JOHN RUSKIN

Rests are an essential part of music. Without rests, the notes would sound chaotic and incoherent, and musicians couldn't complete a performance. Similarly, rest is absolutely necessary to create a harmonious and coherent life. Without adequate rest, we are less productive, less creative, and less healthy. Study after study describes the detrimental effects of not enough sleep and the benefits of adequate rest.

Journey

Today, take a short power nap; ask for guidance around your sleep patterns; or journey or meditate to simply be calm and relaxed.

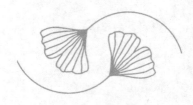

Environmental Supplements

*Both the great forests
and the mountains
live in my bones.
They have taught me,
humbled me, purified me
and changed me.*

—Roshi Joan Halifax

Those of us who are sensitive to the landscapes around us sometimes crave places on the planet. Do you find yourself longing for the cleansing of the beach, the power of the mountains, the protective canopy of the forest, or the expansiveness of the plains? As our physical bodies sometimes crave nutrients or vitamins when we are deficient, our spiritual or energetic bodies can crave places that supply us with something that helps keep us feeling healthy. When we spend time in these places, we soak up their energy and environmental supplements we lack, and can return to our homes invigorated, grounded, soothed—whatever we may need. And remembering the spirit of reciprocity, how can we "feed" these places in return?

Journey

Please advise me about any environmental supplements that would benefit me at this time.

East

We welcome and honor the spirits of the East:
Of beginnings and hope
Of spring and new life.

—Invocation

Acknowledging the directions is part of indigenous cultures from around the world. Before starting ceremonies, and as a daily practice, we can honor the spirit of the directions and welcome them to be present. This can be done silently or with rattling or drumming by facing the direction and giving thanks.*

I was given the invocation above when I asked my helping spirits for guidance about creating my own ceremony for honoring the directions. What is your relationship with the East? Is there an energy or feeling associated with that direction for you? One way to honor East is with a morning greeting.

Journey

Journey to the spirits of the East to ask how you can honor and get to know them better.

---

* More information about honoring the directions is in the Appendix in "Invocation: Welcoming the Spirits and Directions."

Rain

Rain is grace . . .

—John Updike

There are many different kinds of rain: gentle cool spring rain that motivates everything green; warm summer rain that bursts onto the scene in a flash, clearing humidity and amplifying the smell of dark earth and asphalt; blustery fall storms with lashing wind and rain driving sideways, cold and sharp on your face; and then winter—hopefully you get snow, because freezing rain is merciless. What's your favorite way to experience rain? I love the sounds of rain on the roof and how the air and light turn golden after a sweet temperate shower. In all its forms, rain is vital. Let's experience and appreciate rain today.

Journey

Journey and ask to experience rain. Know you are safe in whatever form it comes. Enjoy the rain and thank it for making everything grow.

Open Guidance

*There should be a place
where only the things
you want to happen,
happen.*

—MAURICE SENDAK

Asking specific questions creates a clear intention and is powerful. Today, we balance structure and flow by leaving our question open.

Journey

What do I need to know today?

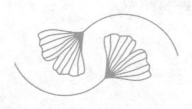

The Science of Silence

The power of nature exists in its silence.
Human words cannot encode the meaning
because human language has access
only to the shadow of meaning.

—MALIDOMA PATRICE SOMÉ

Some of us instinctually know silence is good for us; others find it a little unnerving. The science is behind silence. According to recent research, silence does the following: relaxes us more than "relaxing" music, as measured by the response of blood pressure and circulation in the brain; grows brain cells in the hippocampus, an area associated with learning and memory; heightens abilities to perceive with our other senses; and helps to counteract the increased rates of fatal heart attacks and high blood pressure associated with noise pollution.

Journey

Journey to experience silence today.

Managing Change and Volatility

Cows run away from the storm
while the buffalo charges toward it
—and gets through it quicker.
Whenever I'm confronted with a tough challenge,
I do not prolong the torment,
I become the buffalo.

—WILMA MANKILLER

We welcome, and even initiate, some kinds of changes. Others we do not invite, and these require work to adjust to. While change is inevitable, how we handle it is more under our control. In volatile times with unpredictable changes, it helps to be even more deliberate in our thoughts and actions. Whether we intentionally make changes, or feel as if they are imposed on us, we feel better in the process when we move through them with relative calm, confidence, and good humor.

Journey

Please help me understand and move through the current changes with calm, confidence, and good humor.

Becoming Earth

The mission of all human beings
who achieve consciousness
is to take care of themselves
and mother earth.

—GRANDMOTHER JULIETA CASIMIRO ESTRADA

Let's strengthen our relationship with an aspect of earth today, such as the fertile soil of a garden, the hot sand of the desert, or the mud of a puddle after a spring rain. Pick something that appeals to you or let yourself be guided. Experience yourself as part of the earth. Pay attention to how it feels and whether there is anything about that experience that can help in your life today.

Journey

Journey to merge with an element of the earth. With all your senses, experience what it's like to be earth in this way. Is there anything this aspect of earth wants to communicate to you?

Valuing Time

All things are one thing
and that one thing is all things
—plankton, a shimmering phosphorescence on the sea
and the spinning planets
and an expanding universe,
all bound together by the elastic string of time.
It is advisable to look from the tide pool to the stars
and then back to the tide pool again.

—JOHN STEINBECK

We often think of time as a precious commodity, and talk about "spending it," "wasting it," and "saving it," the same way we talk about money. But you can't accumulate it in the same way; once it passes, it's gone. How we use our valuable time is a reflection on how mindful we are about the things that are meaningful to us. What do you value? How does your relationship with time reflect that? For today, let's ask how to spend it wisely.

Journey

How can I best use my time today?

The Bee

God said to the bee,
"What art thou doing?"
"I am kneading together everything that is good."
—Pyrenean story

Bees, in body and spirit, are a beautiful example of how individuals can relate within a community and be in service to all of life. In many different mythologies, from the Celts' to the Greeks', bees were held sacred and thought to be a bridge between the physical and spiritual realms. They're associated with divination and the Delphic oracle. Bees demonstrate the power of cooperation and collective focus and create remarkable substances, honey, royal jelly, and pollen. Bees are a "keystone species"; because all of nature is dependent on the role they play in pollination, the ecosystem will collapse without them.

Bees are struggling. Colony collapse disorder, a condition where worker honeybees disappear or die, has significantly reduced healthy hives in recent years. If their communities collapse, so may ours. What if we emulated the bees, in their ability to work collectively and to create nourishing healing sweetness for ourselves and others?

Journey

How can I work with bee power to create a healthier world hive?

Quick Calm

My ability to turn good news into anxiety
is rivaled only by my ability
to turn anxiety into chin acne.

—Tina Fey

Practices like meditation, exercise, and prayer can cultivate a more peaceful state of mind over time; however, when a stressful situation takes us by surprise, or we don't have time or space for our usual routine, a quick fix can be helpful to get us through gracefully. In that situation, it's helpful to have a rapid response. In this instance, a rapid response is a way to regain calm quickly without engaging in a longer practice. It may not get you all the way there, but it will tide you over until the crisis moment passes, allowing you to handle it well, rather than in a panicked state. It's like the donut tire that gets you home after a flat but isn't a permanent solution, or the mini first aid kit that has some basics for an emergency, but doesn't compare to your full medicine cabinet.

By definition, this is something you can do with little or no preparation, in a short amount of time, and doesn't require special space or tools.

Journey

How can I find calm quickly in stressful situations?

I Have Everything I Need

Ego says,
"Once everything falls into place, I'll feel peace."
Spirit says,
"Find your peace, and then
everything will fall into place."

—MARIANNE WILLIAMSON

There's always something that's not how we want it to be. This is annoying, right? It creates yearning and a sense of lack. It's easy to slip into thoughts of "If only (fill in the blank) then I would be happy." What if we already have what we need to be happy? If we believe we have everything we need, how would life feel, even if the external circumstances didn't change? "I have everything I need" is one of my favorite mantras; and not because I don't sometimes wish for things that I don't currently have, but because when I reframe my position in relation to what's already there I feel differently. Also, interesting things happen; for example, items that I need (okay, that I want) will occasionally just show up out of the blue. A lovely unworn pair of gloves emerges from the bottom of a drawer just after I say I'd love a pair, or an unexpected check arrives in the mail exactly when it's needed. Try it for yourself.

Journey

Spend time repeating the mantra "I have everything I need." Ask your helping spirits for some reassurance if you want.

Laughter

I would say laughter is the best medicine.
But it's more than that.
It's an entire regime
of antibiotics and steroids.

—STEPHEN COLBERT

Laughing stimulates endorphins and reduces stress and depression. Building it into the day is effective preventive medicine. When I'm sad, if I can laugh ridiculously, I feel better. Being able to see the humor in difficult situations is also a great survival tool. When we take ourselves, or our lives, too seriously it can, well . . . take the fun out of it. Humor is highly subjective, so you decide how to bring it into your life today. Journey to a helping spirit and ask to hear a joke or see a funny scene. In ordinary reality, watch a movie or read something that makes you laugh. Hang out with your goofiest or most hilarious friend.

Journey

Today, do something that makes you laugh.

Animal Spirit Sight

The only true voyage of discovery . . .
would be not to visit strange lands
but to possess other eyes.

—MARCEL PROUST

One of the ways our helping spirits can support us is by showing us a different perspective, one that is detached from our own egoic state. Simply having a new view can be incredibly illuminating.

A power animal may be able to help with this. Not only do they have the distinctly different experience of being in spirit, but they also have the viewpoint of a different kind of being, a nonhuman animal. These two shifts in combination can give you a powerful perspective shift.

Journey

Journey to one of your power animals and ask to see through their eyes.

Mental Health

*The quest for meaning
is the key to mental health
and human flourishing.*

—VIKTOR E. FRANKL

Just like physical health, our mental health benefits from some preventative maintenance. There are many ways to proactively attend to our mental health; walking in the woods, talking to a friend, or making sure to get in a daily workout. Talking to a therapist, doctor, or pastoral counselor can be part of that care. When life is busy or times are stressful, our mental health self-care can fall by the wayside. There may also be ways to take care of ourselves that we haven't thought. Let's check in today.

Journey

How can I best take care of my mental health today?

Feeling Capable

Forget conventionalisms;
forget what the world thinks of you
stepping out of your place;
think your best thoughts,
speak your best words,
work your best works,
looking to your own conscience
for approval.

—SUSAN B. ANTHONY

Whether or not we feel capable significantly affects our confidence. Being capable doesn't mean knowing how to do everything. It means being equipped to manage the challenges that life presents you, through your own knowledge or creativity, the ability to seek help, find new information, or simply troubleshoot as needed. When we feel capable of handling life, it actually becomes more manageable, even when it is hard.

Journey

Journey for ways to increase your feeling of being capable.

Unexpected Kindness

To give pleasure to a single heart
by a single act
is better than 10,000 heads
bowing in prayer.

—MAHATMA GANDHI

Rather than asking for a *specific* way that kindness is needed today, let's ask that we be attuned to recognize *wherever and whenever* kindness is needed today.

Journey

Journey and ask for help in being attuned to wherever and whenever kindness is needed today.

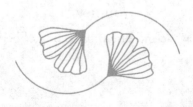

Nourishing Foods

One cannot think well,
love well,
sleep well,
if one has not dined well.

—Virginia Woolf

Food is fuel. The quality and quantity of fuel affects how we run. Some foods are almost universally good for us. Others may be most useful occasionally, seasonally, when your body is in a particular state (like fighting a cold), or when you need some comfort. Food feeds us physically and also psychologically; our psychological state impacts our health and vice versa.

Journey

What foods does my body need today to be strong and healthy?

Love Manifesting Love

Omnia vincit amor.

—Virgil

Does being loving generate more love? I think it does, and not only as manifest in the original interaction, but in subsequent interactions in an exponentially increasing and expanding way. This is particularly true if the acts of loving-kindness are unexpected or extraordinary. For example, if during a time of need someone who had no obligation to be so was kind or generous to you, there is a high likelihood that you will shift how you engage others, not just one other, but *many* subsequent others. The loving-kindness multiplies. Even if all of the people in the second tier aren't moved to "pay it forward," the overall amount of love goes up because many people will, and it keeps spreading. How might you be ground zero for a wave of love and kindness today?

Journey

Journey about ways to be surprisingly loving today.

Initiations

We take spiritual initiation
when we become conscious
of the Divine within us,
and thereby contact
the Divine without us.

—DION FORTUNE

Initiations take many forms. Some are the typical rites of passage that mark changes in our lives: birth, coming of age, graduation, marriage, death. These milestones are often stressful, joyful, and painful, and they push us into new phases of understanding and capability. Other experiences can be initiations, too, and get less acknowledgment as the commencements that they are: failures and successes, illnesses and healings, dark nights of the soul and spiritual awakenings, breakdowns and breakthroughs. Let's ask for insight about any unrealized initiations you've experienced in your life and honor them for what they are.

Journey

Please reveal to me any unrealized initiations, so that I can honor them and myself for surviving and learning from the experience.

Future Self

The ceremonies were about
what all our ancestors were doing
for the future,
for future use.
We didn't know back then
it meant today.

—GRANDMOTHER RITA PITKA BLUMENSTEIN

I've often thought about going back in time with the information I have now to have a word with my younger self. Mostly I want to give her a hug and some reassurance; I've got some information that would be really useful! What if it was possible to receive information from our future selves now?

Journey

Journey and ask for help receiving a message from your future self.

Honoring Your Body

If we are creating ourselves all the time,
then it is never too late
to begin creating the bodies we want
instead of the ones
we mistakenly assume
we are stuck with.

—DEEPAK CHOPRA

We are incredibly hard on our bodies. We rely on them for everything from the most basic functions of life (breathing, speaking, moving), to the most nuanced experiences (gently rocking a baby to sleep, adding the finishing details to a painting, performing neurosurgery). Many people are critical of the bodies they have, focusing on what they don't like or what isn't functioning perfectly. Today, let's appreciate all the amazing functions our physical bodies perform every day, often without us giving them a second thought.

Journey

Journey to appreciate your physical body. Pick one particular part of your body, or your body as a whole. While journeying, flood your body with gratitude.

Healing Springs

There is something very shamanic
in the Celt's respect
for the spring or well
as a portal into the Otherworld.

—Tom Cowan

Springs are places of power. The water of natural springs can have physical healing properties and springs are often connected to spiritual healing as well. They are also thin spots, places where the spiritual worlds are more accessible. In mythology, they are often associated with aspects of the divine. For example, Brigid (celebrated by Pagans and Catholics alike) is known for her healing spring.

Journey

Journey to a sacred healing spring and request a healing from the waters.

Overcoming Fear

The very cave you are afraid to enter
turns out to be the source
of what you are looking for.

—Joseph Campbell

What are you afraid of? Some fears are specific (heights, snakes), others more vague (the future, not meeting the expectations of others). We are all afraid of something. Yet, feeling afraid can be a source of shame or anxiety for many. Addressing fear openly—even just with our own spiritual support network—can help to dispel the power fear has over us.

Journey

What am I afraid of? Please help me overcome my fear.

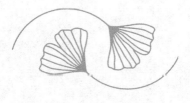

Strengths

Success is achieved by developing our strengths,
not by eliminating our weaknesses.

—Marilyn vos Savant

Are you more likely to dwell on your weaknesses or your strengths? Today's journey is for everyone, and particularly for those who have a tendency to remember their faults or failures in excruciating detail and forget their strengths or accomplishments. Research shows that when we focus on our strengths, rather than our weaknesses, and apply those strengths deliberately to different life situations, we have greater hope, work engagement, authentic self-expression, and well-being.

Journey

What are some of my strengths I should be reminded of today? How can I best apply them in my life?

In the Wind

I converse with the wind.
Everything is air.
I call the wind as God.
They sit with us
and they sit on my tongue
and they speak through me.

—Grandmother Aama Bambo

Have you ever opened up the windows in your home and let the breeze blow through? Or stood outside on a windy day and felt the air rushing around you? The change in the way a space feels, or the way our bodies feel, after being surrounded by moving air is tangible. The elements are powerful helpers in our own healing, and they take many forms. Wind is one form of the element air and is particularly helpful in cleansing and clearing, both on the physical and energetic levels. Let's ask to experience ourselves as wind today, embodying the power to purify whatever and wherever we are.

Journey

Journey to experience yourself as wind. Let go of anything that needs to be swept away.

Service at Home

Shifting focus
from self to relationship
brings forth the understanding
that giving is the most satisfying gift.

—BRADFORD KEENEY

We play different roles in the varying circles we move through: home, work, social, community. We're called to help in different ways, such as taking an active role, being a steadying presence, or even stepping back and letting someone else have the opportunity to step up. Today, ask for guidance about your role at home.

Journey

How can I best serve at home today?

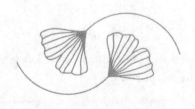

Fairy Magic

*I think that people
who can't believe in fairies
aren't worth knowing.*

—TORI AMOS

"Fairy tales" are synonymous with children's stories, but lore about fairies and fairy magic is not always playful and sweet; fairies are complicated and not to be trifled with. Some folks build tiny houses to honor them or leave offerings to appease or attract them. Do you believe in fairies? Have you witnessed them? If it appeals to you to have more fairy energy in your life, ask for some guidance about how to do that in a suitable way.

Journey

Journey for guidance about your relationship with fairies.

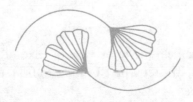

Awakening Wisdom: Ancestors

I am thankful for this Holy Mother,
our planet the Earth,
who received all of us,
for the destiny we have here
to be this channel for eternal life
in receiving the knowledge
from our ancestors
to give to future generations.

—GRANDMOTHER MARIA ALICE CAMPOS FREIRE

We are part of a long chain of human beings that stretches backward in time and will unfurl forward. Finding our place in that continuum and considering the different kinds of knowledge that people of all ages possess helps us be truly wise. We can learn from those who came before; we benefit from the length and breadth of their experiences and from the perspective they bring to today. Truly sage elders use that perspective of time to inform their decisions and ways of being. How might we learn from them?

Journey

Spirits, please help me to be wise in relation to my ancestors. And help me see where I can learn from those who are older than me.

Awakening Wisdom: Descendants

*We do not inherit the earth
from our ancestors;
we borrow it from our children*
—CHIEF SEATTLE

In the last journey we focused on wisdom in relation to our ancestors. We can also learn from those much younger than us, who come with fresh energy, unencumbered by accumulated fear, hopeful, and open to new experiences. The young are better at adapting to a world with a faster rate of change than any who have come before. It's easy for people of any age (ahem, teens) to feel like they are more savvy (substitute wise, cool, responsible, sensible, if that makes more sense to you) than someone from a previous generation. To be truly wise we need to consider the different kinds of wisdom that people of all ages possess.

Journey

Spirits, please help me to be wise in relation to my descendants. And help me see where I can learn from those who are younger than me.

Unhealthy Habits

Habit is habit,
and not to be flung out of the window by any man,
but coaxed downstairs
one step at a time.

—MARK TWAIN

Habits form over time and with repetition. Willpower alone often doesn't work to change a habit. Research shows new ways of thinking combined with repatterning of behavior, can. You don't have any unhealthy habits, do you? Well, just in case you do, today is the day to ask for help in changing them.

Journey

Please give me guidance and help around changing my habit of _____.

Healing Stories

*Stories can function
as a kind of hypnosis.
They help people's mind
to prepare for healing.*

—Lewis Mehl-Madrona, MD

Words can inspire us and take us down. We are constantly communicating with ourselves internally, and the words and stories we choose are just as powerful as the words and stories others may speak to us out loud. What are some words that would inspire you today? What would a healing story convey to you right now?

Journey

Please tell me a healing story that will inspire me today.

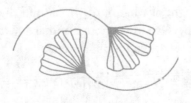

Natural Rhythms

A human body can think thoughts,
play a piano, kill germs, remove toxins,
make a baby all at once.
Once it's doing that
your biological rhythms are actually mirroring
the symphony of the universe
because you have circadian rhythms,
seasonal rhythms, tidal rhythms . . .
they mirror everything that is happening
in the whole universe.

—MICHIO KAKU

Have you ever tried to get a loved one jazzed up about something in the morning—to go out, take a walk, do something fun, go to work, whatever—if they are really not a "morning person"? Not a fun experience for either party, right? That same person at 11 p.m. may be filled with energy and enthusiasm, while you are drooping and cranky, ready to hit the bed. When we work with our natural rhythms, rather than against them, everything flows more easily; however, we can lose sight of what our own natural rhythms are and get out of sync. When we notice and attune to our natural cycles, life generally functions better.

Journey

Journey and ask, "How can I work with my natural cycles most effectively?"

Pause to Rest

And whenever we pause and enter the quiet,
and rest in the utter stillness,
we can hear that whispering voice
calling to us still:
never forget the Good, and never forget the True,
and never forget the Beautiful,
for these are the faces
of your own deepest Self,
freely shown to you.

—KEN WILBER

Whether it's extra sleep or gentle activities that nourish and replenish you, pausing your usual routine to rest is healing.

There are different kinds of rest, so for the *Rest* journeys, pick from one of these options: While journeying, go to a place in non-ordinary reality that you love and rest there. You can invite your power animal to be with you, but rather than asking questions or seeking something, just find a place to be at ease and relax. Or, take this day to skip the practice and use the time to have a short nap or period of stillness, not asking anything of your body or mind.

Journey

For your experience of rest today, pick from one of the options above.

Grief

Should you shield the canyons
from the windstorm,
you would never see
the beauty of their carvings.

—Elisabeth Kübler Ross

There is no exact formula for grieving. The process is variable, hard to measure, often difficult to talk about, and can span many years. It can feel easier to shove it down than deal with it directly. Even if the grief cannot be fully resolved, sometimes it's healthy for it to be addressed more openly.

Journey

Please help me with any unresolved grief that needs to come to the surface.

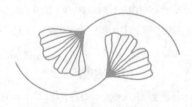

Space

You don't need a new life,
just a new lens
through which to view the one you have.

—MARIANNE WILLIAMSON

Imagine yourself in space. You're surrounded by stillness and stark beauty. The indigo darkness is a dramatic backdrop for the crisp brilliance of stars and planets. Just be there and relax in this profound and otherworldly environment, so close and yet so far away from our own.

Journey

Ask one of your helping spirits to take you high into the environment of outer space. Know that you have everything you need to be comfortable and safe. What is it like to have this shift of perspective in relation to Earth, to be weightless, to be in silence?

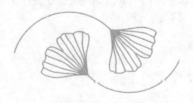

Sensual Enjoyment

To be sensual, I think,
is to respect and rejoice in the force of life,
of life itself,
and to be present in all that one does,
from the effort of loving
to the breaking of bread.

—JAMES BALDWIN

Enjoying our senses is one of the best parts of being human. Smelling bread baking, watching a radiant sunset, petting warm silky cat fur, tasting your favorite food, feeling a cool breeze on your skin, or cuddling with your beloved. As we seek connection to our spiritual selves, let's remember to appreciate the joys of our physical selves as well.

Journey

Journey to a helping spirit and ask to become particularly attuned to the pleasurable perceptions of your senses today. As you go about your day, pay extra attention to the enjoyment of your senses.

Thank You

If the only prayer you ever said
was thank you
that would be enough.

—MEISTER ECKHARDT

In our prayers and journeys we tend to ask for things. Today, let's just say thank you to our helping spirits, God, the universe, however you relate to the divine. Consider creating something to honor a helping presence in your life.

Journey

Journey to say thank you to the divine. For example, you can do this by visiting a helping spirit and telling them why you are appreciative, by offering a prayer of thanks to the divinity of the natural world, or by holding a state of gratitude for the vastness of God or source energy.

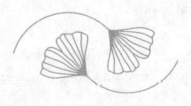

Healing Movement

If we seek the real source of the dance,
if we go to nature, we find that
the dance of the future
is the dance of the past,
the dance of eternity,
and has been and always will be the same . . .
The movement of waves,
of winds, of the earth
is ever the same lasting harmony.

—ISADORA DUNCAN

Movement is an integral part of life, from the micro level of our cellular functions to the macro level of the seasonally shifting patterns of the environment. In our bodies, movement stimulates synovial fluid to flush the tissues of our joints, keeping them flexible. On the Earth, the movement of air and ocean currents prevents stagnation and helps plant and animal life breathe, reproduce, and migrate effectively. Movement sustains individual and environmental health.

Journey

Journey and ask, "How can I bring movement into my life for healing?"

Hard to Love

Love is life.
All, everything that I understand,
I understand only because I love.
Everything is, everything exists,
only because I love.
Everything is united by it alone.
Love is God, and to die means
that I, a particle of love,
shall return to the general and eternal source.

—LEO TOLSTOY

Feeling love is easy when the objects of our affection are easy. For example, if you're a dog lover and I say to you "Think of a dog and feel love in your heart," it's not hard, right? However, if you were bitten by a dog as a child, and never had a close relationship with a dog, this may be hard. If you adore your parents, and I say "Send love to your parents today," no problem. If your parents were cruel, or abandoned you, it's a problem. Think of something or someone that is a challenge for you to love and send love their way. If this feels too hard, think of one simple or easy aspect of that individual and focus on that at first.

Journey

Send love to something or someone you find hard to love.

Gift of Loneliness

If you go deeper and deeper
into your own heart,
you'll be living in a world
with less fear, isolation and loneliness.

—SHARON SALZBERG

We generally think of loneliness as a negative state. As with many situations that cause stress or pain, how we handle loneliness can make all the difference. Are you feeling lonely right now, or are there times in your life when you've felt lonely? Most of us have, but has loneliness ever taught you anything, or could it? Could it bolster your self-reliance? If it pushed your willingness to be vulnerable or to accept help from others, might that ultimately create less loneliness? Let's ask for guidance about loneliness today, either insight into how it may have served you in the past or how you can work with it right now.

Journey

Please give me help and guidance about loneliness.

Kindness to Wildlife

Animals make us human.

—Temple Grandin

It's generally easy to be kind to the animals we have intentionally welcomed into our lives and homes. What about wild animals, like the deer who eats your flowers or the bat who gets in your attic? Let's journey on ways to be kind to wildlife today, both the ones we encounter face-to-face and the ones who are affected by our actions from many steps removed, such as sea creatures dealing with plastic trash.

Journey

Journey about ways to be kind to wildlife.

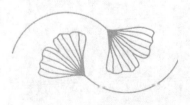

What Needs Hearing?

So many of us are reaching out,
hoping someone out there
will grab our hands and remind us
we are not as alone as we fear.

—Roxane Gay

What we ask is naturally bound to our awareness. When we ask to be told what we need to hear, we give the helping spirits permission to provide guidance beyond the scope of what we may conceive of asking them. This can be surprising and powerful.

Journey

Please tell me what I need to hear.

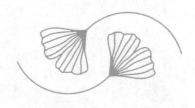

Warming Sun

The Sun,
the hearth of affection and life,
pours burning love
on the delighted earth.

—Arthur Rimbaud

Today, let's enjoy the simple yet luxurious pleasure of the warmth of the sun on our faces (without having to worry about UV rays). As you envision yourself lying on the beach or in a meadow, or sitting on a cozy chair on your patio, or paddling by in a canoe, lift your face to the sun, close your eyes, and absorb the healing glow of the sun's rays as they warm your skin to the perfect temperature.

Journey

Journey to experience the warmth of the sun on your face.

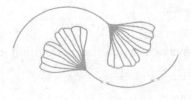

Dreaming a New Dream

In the practice of shamanism,
life is seen as a dream.
What you daydream about
while going to work,
taking walks, eating and so on,
also reflects and helps create
the life you are now living
and how you are contributing
to the events we're witnessing on the planet.

—SANDRA INGERMAN

Historically, it was the shaman's job to dream on behalf of the community, to have a vision for the collective that was nourishing and sustaining, to dream the world into being. When ordinary reality was not going well, they needed to dream a new dream for their community. We are in one of those times. But it's not just the shamans who are able to dream. We all help dream our world into being. What would an ideal world look like to you?

Journey

Journey to experience a new dream or vision for your world.

Building Bridges

Be kind to bad and good,
for you don't know your own heart.

—Sarah Winnemucca

Physical bridges span places that once seemed impossible to cross. There are other kinds of bridges, too, ones that help us reach across less tangible barriers. A smile can bridge barriers of despair or loneliness. An encouraging or kind word can break down the walls of insecurity or fear. Where can you build bridges in your life today?

Journey

Journey to ask, "Where can I build bridges today?"

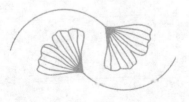

Boundaries of Forgiveness

God said there is only abundance,
and the only way through is to forgive. . . .
Our healing is not just for ourselves,
it is for the universe.
We forget who we are,
and that is the cause of our illness.

—Grandmother Rita Pitka Blumenstein

What does forgiveness mean to you? Energetically, forgiveness is more about letting go than actually giving someone absolution. It's also reasonable and healthy to maintain your personal boundaries. You can be forgiving without subjecting yourself to unacceptable behavior. The line can be a challenging one to find and sustain.

Journey

Please give me more clarity around forgiveness and boundaries.

Moderation

Everything in moderation,
including moderation.

—Oscar Wilde

What's your take on moderation? Depending on your natural temperament, it may help keep you on track, or it may be overrated. If you are naturally temperate, intense emotion or swift action periodically may be just what you need. If, on the other hand, you tend toward the extreme already, temperance may help you avoid swinging like a pendulum and having to work to pull yourself into balance on a regular basis. Let's ask for some guidance about moderation.

Journey

Please give me some guidance about moderation today.

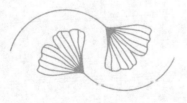

Starlight

My father would tell me
how the Creator
loved us so much
that he gave us a star
and the star was the fire,
so we are the Star People.

—GRANDMOTHER MARGARET BEHAN

Glittering starlight is a gift to us on Earth, a celestial work of art that we get to enjoy many nights. What if you were in the middle of the display? Today's journey is to become the starlight.

Journey

Envision yourself journeying upward into the night sky. Transform from flesh to light, maybe by unzipping your human form and stepping out, leaving your physical self behind as you temporarily become the sparkling beauty of starlight.

Unwelcome Thoughts

Our mind is what
we have to be really happy within.
If everyone really did
a true spiritual practice,
which develops a positive mind,
the world would not be in
the dire situation
we find it in today.
—GRANDMOTHER TSERING DOLMA GYALTONG

It's easy for some kinds of thoughts to become burdensome. Like annoying and long-winded guests who stay too long at the party, unwelcome thoughts are loud, self-centered, and suck the air out of the room, leaving little space for other conversation. Today, let's politely and firmly thank them for coming, show them out the door, and return to the peace of your quiet internal space.

Journey

Journey to show unwelcome thoughts out the door.

Self-Compassion

With self-compassion,
we give ourselves
the same kindness and care
we'd give to a good friend.

—Kristen Neff

Compassion for other beings is beneficial all around. Research shows that practicing meditation focusing on compassion for someone else helps *us* to feel better, and yet we so often find it hardest to be compassionate to ourselves. Being self-compassionate does not mean that we indulge in self-pity or become self-absorbed or narcissistic. It simply means that we are reasonably kind and gentle with ourselves.

Journey

Be compassionate with yourself today. Ask for guidance if this is challenging.

Journeying Through Time

Take care how you place
your moccasins upon the Earth,
step with care, for the faces
of the future generations
are looking up from the Earth
waiting their turn for life.

—WILMA MANKILLER

Do you think it's possible to connect with our future selves? What if you could send love and appreciation to that older, hopefully wiser, version of yourself? It might be like a sweet note that got lost in the mail for a while that you receive just when you need it most.

Journey

Journey and ask for help in sending a loving message to your future self.

Roses

Beauty is an ecstasy;
it is as simple as hunger.
There is really nothing to be said about it.
It is like the perfume of a rose:
you can smell it and that is all.

—W. SOMERSET MAUGHAM

We appreciate roses for the physical beauty of their extravagant colors, elegant form, and heavenly scent. They also have a long history as metaphysical symbols of divinity, feminine power, love, creativity, and even secrecy. Today, let us acknowledge the loveliness embodied in these flowers, and also recognize the important role they have played in our collective religious, civic, and cultural heritage. You can journey to be in a rose garden and simply enjoy the colors and smells, or you can ask for information about using rose oil for healing, or about how the symbolism of the rose is relevant in your life now. As usual, let the helping spirits give you the gift of what is most needed.

Journey

Journey to experience and honor the rose.

Signs in Nature

We Indians think of the earth
and the whole universe
as a never-ending circle,
and in this circle man is just another animal.
The buffalo and the coyote are our brothers,
the birds, our cousins.
Even the tiniest ant, even a louse,
even the smallest flower you can find
—they are all relatives.

—JENNY LEADING CLOUD

Part of seeing with shaman's eyes is to experience nature as a source of information and guidance. As we are an integral part of the natural world, our movements affect and are affected by the other beings around us. By paying attention to the elements, animals, and plants, and their interactions with you, you can develop the ability to interpret the signs in nature.

Journey

Think of a question. Ask for help in divining an answer by observing the natural world as you move through your day. Remember that information is often presented symbolically. Consider creative ways to interpret what you see outside today.

Regret

Mistakes are a fact of life.
It is the response to error that counts.

—Nikki Giovanni

Do you regret anything about your past? Our past choices can have profound implications for our lives, and it is easy to get stuck on "what if," "if only," and regrets about the past. Regret itself isn't very useful unless we use it as fuel to make better choices today.

Journey

Journey for guidance about letting go of regret.

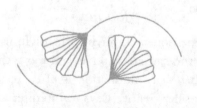

South

We call in and honor the spirits of the South:
Of fertility and creativity
Of warmth and abundance.

—Invocation

Acknowledging the directions is part of indigenous cultures from around the world. Before starting ceremonies, and as a daily practice, we can honor the spirit of the directions and welcome them to be present. This can be done silently or with rattling or drumming by facing the direction and giving thanks.*

I was given the invocation above when I asked my helping spirits for guidance about creating my own ceremony for honoring the directions. What is your relationship with the South? Is there an energy or feeling associated with that direction for you? One way to honor South is with a noon greeting.

Journey

Journey to the spirits of the South to ask how you can honor and get to know them better.

---

* More information about honoring the directions is in the Appendix in "Invocation: Welcoming the Spirits and Directions."

When Things Fall Apart

*Every act of creation
is first an act of destruction.*

—Pablo Picasso

When things don't go as planned, and not in a good way, panic can set in. We don't make the best decisions when we are filled with fear. Let's ask for a method to use to calm down when things appear to be falling apart.

Journey

Journey and ask for a way to stay calm when things appear to be falling apart.

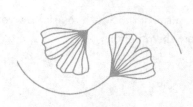

Healthy Vulnerability

To be fully alive,
fully human,
and completely awake
is to be continually thrown
out of the nest.

—Pema Chödrön

Vulnerability opens doors. What it opens doors *to* scares the heck out of us. We've all been hurt, and we tend to associate pain with times when we were vulnerable. Vulnerability is also the precursor to most forms of meaningful interaction, such as love, accomplishment, intimacy, compassion, perseverance, delight, and tenderness. Where could you use more of it in your life?

Journey

Journey and ask, "Where would vulnerability be helpful in my life now?"

Getting It Done

To achieve goals you've never achieved before,
you need to start doing things
you've never done before.

—STEPHEN COVEY

What needs to get done today? Does anything feel heavy or daunting? Where could you use a boost to push through and do what you need to do? If you know what this thing is, ask for it specifically, or simply ask for general assistance in getting through today with grace.

Journey

Journey and say, "Spirits, thank you for helping me get it done today."

Water

If there is magic on this planet,
it is contained in water.

—Tristan Gooley

We *are* water. Water is virtually everywhere: in the air, in our bodies, in the ground, in our food. Without it, we die very quickly. Many of us don't have to give it much thought though; turn the tap, out it comes, and hot or cold no less! We flock to the ocean and lakeshores and waterfalls, seeking the beauty that water affords us. Today, let's make an effort to appreciate and cultivate a harmonious relationship with water.

Journey

Journey to the spirit of water and ask for guidance about relating to water in a harmonious way.

Point of Birth

You have to figure out who you are,
and who you are isn't about
what job you have or
what kind of car you drive.
You have to think hard
about what really matters to you.

—ELIZABETH WARREN

We are born into this life as potential, a blueprint with possibilities. Then life happens. Let's ask if there is anything from your blueprint that would be helpful to be reminded of today.

Journey

Journey to ask your helping spirits to remind you about something helpful from the blueprint you were born with.

Human Love

Love is or it ain't.
Thin love ain't love at all.

—Toni Morrison

Who do you love? Today is about radiating love for another person. It can be romantic love, parental love, love for a friend, love for a teacher or inspirational person. Choose someone and simply feel love for them.

Journey

Sink into your feelings of love for another human being.

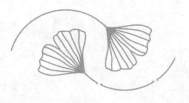

Stone

The stone contains the history,
past and future,
of mankind linked to all else.

—CLAUDE PONCELET

When it feels like the Earth is shifting precariously under your feet, and it's hard to find firm footing, a big rock can help—literally and energetically. The energy of stone is ancient and slow. We can draw from it to help find stability in chaotic times.

Journey

Journey to connect with the energy of stone to find slow, steady calm.

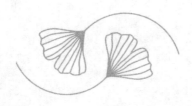

Back in Time
to Love Yourself as a Baby

Our thoughts and emotions
overlap and intermingle,
and this mixing of head and heart
connects us to future events
hidden in the dark womb of time.

—BARBARA TEDLOCK, PhD

Babies are meant to be adored. Whether you were showered with love and affection, suffered from neglect, or had an experience somewhere in between, let's take a trip back in time today.

Journey

Journey and ask to be shown yourself as a baby. Hold baby you and love yourself tenderly, fiercely, and unconditionally.

Your Living Space

Where thou art,
that is home.

—EMILY DICKINSON

How do you relate to the space in which you live? Do you love and appreciate it, or do you complain about it? Have you settled in so every surface reflects your personality, or do you use it like a hotel room? Our living spaces provide a container for us, and they have their own energy with which we interact. They also deserve some credit for hosting us; regardless of our mood, our level of attentiveness, or how dirty we let them get, they are always there for us. Let's express appreciation for our living space today.

Journey

Journey to honor your living space. This is a Middle World journey. Simply "walk out" into your space and see what it is like. Are there particular places in your home that need some love and attention? Maybe the whole place is thirsty for a little gratitude. Ask your helping spirits for guidance as needed.

Speak Up, Stay Quiet

Keep the other person's well being in mind
when you feel an attack of
soul-purging truth coming on.

—Betty White

When is it time to speak our minds and when is it best to keep our thoughts to ourselves? This line can be a fine one, but the decision to be vocal or not can have big repercussions in our lives and relationships. Today, let's explore where we could be more discerning around this topic. Are there times when we need to be more assertive and outspoken, on our own behalf or for the sake of others? Conversely, do we need to hold our tongues a little more often, or in particular situations?

Journey

Please guide me about when I should speak up and when I should keep my thoughts to myself.

Play in Nature

*Trees are very social beings
and they help each other out.*

—PETER WOHLLEBEN

Play in nature today. Being outside is healing in and of itself, and playing outside is even better. One of my favorite mornings was spent playing in a giant leaf pile with my daughter and then relaxing, entirely submerged except for my face, looking up at the trees. Roll in the grass, chase fireflies, climb a tree, or frolic in the waves. Take advantage of what nature has to offer you today, in ordinary and nonordinary reality.

Journey

Play in nature. Ideally, make some time to do this in ordinary reality as well as within your journey.

Flow

You go into flow
when your highest strengths are deployed
to meet the highest challenges
that come your way.

—Martin Seligman

If you've had a flow moment, you know how satisfying they are; you are utterly engaged, time melts away, you're focused but not stressed, the rest of the world seems to align with you or fade out, you glide through whatever you are doing smoothly and enjoyably. Yeah, let's do that.

Journey

Spirits, thank you for helping me get into the flow. Guidance accepted and appreciated.

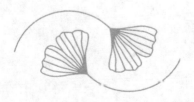

Bird's-Eye View

*Parrots have been known
to teach other parrots
to talk smack.*

—Jennifer Ackerman

Many birds are smart and have very distinct personalities, despite some of our early cultural stereotypes about them, like the expression "birdbrain." How do you relate to our feathered family? Do you enjoy watching songbirds cluster colorfully at the feeder, or a hawk soaring smoothly overhead? Have you had dreams of flying? Maybe you don't pay much attention to birds at all. Whatever relationship you've had with birds to this point, let's get a perspective shift.

Journey

Journey and ask to experience the world from a bird's eyes.

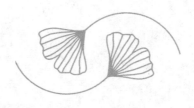

Violet

The violets in the mountains
have broken through the rocks . . .
—Tennessee Williams

Violet is beautiful and powerful; violet light is a powerful tool in spiritual healing. The crown chakra is violet and connects us to the higher realms of divinity. The lovely heart-shaped flower was a symbol of ancient Athens and was associated with love. The bloom also contains medicinal properties. In ancient times, garlands of violets were worn to prevent headaches; we now know that they contain salicylic acid, the basis of aspirin. They are also delicious and make a lovely dye. As with many flowering plants, especially small wild ones, there is much going on beneath the surface, and their outer beauty is a reflection of something deeper and more meaningful.

Journey

Journey to appreciate violet in any or all forms.

Grounding

We recognized a long time ago
that there was life all around us—
in the water, in the ground, in the vegetation.
Children were introduced to the elements
so that as we grew up,
we were not looking down upon nature
or looking up to nature.

—BEAR HEART

What does it mean to "ground" yourself? In electrical terms, the ground wire is a way for current to return safely to the Earth, rather than causing a short to the system or, worse, a fire. Similarly, when we ground ourselves energetically, we allow any extra energy that may have built up to return safely to the Earth or dissipate harmlessly. Energy that builds up in our bodies can lead to physical symptoms (headaches, stomachaches), emotional symptoms (anxiety, depression) and mental symptoms (lack of focus, poor memory). Simply sitting on the Earth can be grounding, and so can imagining yourself lying down somewhere in nature. Ask your helping spirits for a way to ground that is particularly suited to you.

Journey

Please give me a good method for grounding.

Attracting Kindness

One who knows how
to show and to accept kindness
will be a friend
better than any possession.

—SOPHOCLES

Are you open to receiving the kindness of others? Do you generally expect it, or are you usually prepared for its absence? Sometimes the more open and receptive we are to receiving something, the more likely it flows our way.

Journey

Journey to ask for help in attracting and receiving kindness from other people.

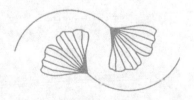

Rest and Rejuvenation

Rest is the sweet sauce of labor.

—Plutarch

Getting enough rest is critical to the functioning of our bodies and minds. Rest helps you restore yourself and replenish what is spent over time.

There are different kinds of rest, so for the Rest journeys, pick from one of these options: While journeying, go to a place in non-ordinary reality that you love and rest there. You can invite your power animal to be with you, but rather than asking questions or seeking something, just find a place to be at ease and relax. Or, take this day to skip the practice and use the time to have a short nap or period of stillness, not asking anything of your body or mind.

Journey

However you need it today—rest, relax, and rejuvenate.

Answers

Your worst enemy
is your best teacher.

—THE BUDDHA

Do you have a question (issue, problem, dilemma) that you've been mulling over for a while with seemingly no progress toward an answer? Today is the day to address it. Try to clear your mind of your past deliberations. Turn this question over to your helping spirits.

As you journey, try to be as open and receptive as possible to whatever you are shown, whatever you hear, whatever sensations you have in your body. When you return, write, record, draw, or in some way document it as thoroughly as possible *without* trying to come to a conclusion. Let it sit a while. Then come back and review and see what insights you have about your question.

Journey

What is the answer to my question?

Service at Work

When people go to work,
they shouldn't have to leave their hearts at home.

—Betty Bender

We play different roles in the varying circles we move through—home, work, social, and community. We're called to help in different ways, such as taking an active role, being a steadying presence, or even stepping back and letting someone else have the opportunity to step up. Today, we ask for guidance about your role at work.

Journey

How can I best serve at work today?

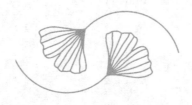

Breathe In, Breathe Out

Another glorious day,
the air as delicious to the lungs
as nectar to the tongue.

—JOHN MUIR

The word "inspire," which we now generally associate with a creative, or even divine, influence or insight, has its origins in the Latin *inspirare*, "to breathe or blow into." Breath is life. Because breathing is part of your autonomic system, you don't need to pay attention to it most of the time; however, you can intentionally use breath to make changes to your physical and emotional bodies.

A few deep breaths will calm you down. Breathing rhythmically for a few moments helps in meditation. In daily life, and particularly in stressful times, it's common to resort to shallow breathing or even to holding your breath for short periods. This compounds the state of tension. As you journey to ask for guidance about your breathing today, also pay attention to your breath, keeping it steady and deep.

Journey

Journey and ask for guidance about how to use your breath optimally.

Shame and Guilt

If we can share our story
with someone who responds
with empathy and understanding,
shame can't survive.

—Brené Brown

Ugh. I don't want to talk about it. I'm sure you don't, either. And it's often why shame and guilt become insidious parts of our inner dialogue. We are reluctant to speak out loud about things we feel ashamed of, or guilty about. Whether it's related to our behaviors, our bodies, our pasts, or our likes and dislikes, shame and guilt make us uncomfortable. They tend to fester. Let's start the process of bringing these areas to light, at least internally, so their hold over us can be released.

Journey

Ask for help in identifying areas where you feel shame and/or guilt. Ask for help in healing around those issues.

Faith

The thing always happens
that you really believe in;
and the belief in a thing
makes it happen.

—Frank Lloyd Wright

What does faith mean to you? Is it believing in something for which you have no evidence? Or is it unshakable confidence? Maybe both. Faith is a powerful force that can fortify us in challenging times and provide a solid framework for living. There are also potential pitfalls when it is misplaced. Today, let's journey on the concept of faith.

Journey

What is faith's role in my life now, and is it a balanced one?

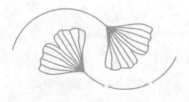

Pure Joy

Beauty is the experience
that gives us a sense of joy
and a sense of peace
simultaneously.

—Rollo May

What brings you joy? When do you experience pure enjoyment that makes the world fade away? If you know what this is, try to experience some of it today, even if it is internal; for example, if skiing brings you joy, and it's June in North Carolina, do a journey where you experience yourself skiing. Or if what brings you joy is your grandchildren or your puppies and you are not with them right now, do a full sensory meditation where you see them, hold them, smell them, talk to them, etc. Let's celebrate the ways we can find joy in our lives, from the profound and communal, to the simple and deeply personal. In addition to your journey, try to take a practical step to bring joy into your life today.

Journey

Journey to experience joy today.

Freedom

*My own Lakota language was finally
cut out of my mind because we would get
punished if we ever spoke of it.*

—GRANDMOTHER RITA
LONG VISITOR HOLY DANCE

Gratitude practices can be powerful, especially when we really look at things we're so accustomed to that they're practically invisible. While those differ for each of us, most Americans today do not have to experience some things that were common not that long ago, such as being enslaved by another person. The practice of shamanism itself was illegal in many places, including the United States, and until quite recently punishable by jail or worse. Today, let's think about the lack of freedom our ancestors of various religions and ethnicities faced, and what many of our brothers and sisters today are still facing.

Journey

In today's journey, let's give thanks for our freedoms, and see those without them in their divine light. Perhaps ask your helping spirits for some practical advice about how to be a positive force for change in this area.

Open Guidance

*There is no benefit in worrying
whatsoever.*

—THE DALAI LAMA

Asking specific questions creates a clear intention and is powerful. Today, we balance structure and flow by leaving our question open.

Journey

What do I need to know today?

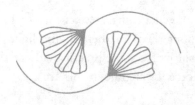

Healing Garden

I have seen in my patients
the restorative and healing powers
of nature and gardens. . . .
In many cases,
gardens and nature
are more powerful than any medication.

—OLIVER SACKS

Previously, you journeyed to your ideal garden sanctuary. Your garden is a place to visit regularly: to plant, tend, and watch grow, to relax and just enjoy. Let's return to your healing garden today. How is it doing? Tend it and then let it tend to you.

Journey

Journey to your healing garden. Spend time soaking up its healing energy.

Last Day

I wake up every morning thinking . . .
this is my last day.
And I jam everything into it.
There's no time for mediocrity.
This is no damned dress rehearsal.

—ANITA RODDICK

If this were your last day, how would you want to spend it? Who would you want to be with? Would you feel mostly complete or are there loose ends that need attention? Are amends due to anyone? Hopefully this is not your last day, yet unresolved relationships or lingering tasks can weigh disproportionately heavy on the present. Let's ask for guidance about lightening your load now, so whether you have one day or thousands you feel free when the time comes.

Journey

Is there anything lingering I should address now?

Love in the Present

People look at me
like I'm a little strange,
when I go around talking to squirrels
and rabbits and stuff.
That's OK. That's just OK.

—Bob Ross

Journey and experience yourself right now, wherever you are, whatever you are feeling. What kind words do you need to hear? Be gentle and loving to yourself.

Journey

Journey to send love to yourself in the present moment.

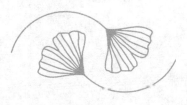

Sacrifice

A basic law:
the more you practice the art of thankfulness,
the more you have to be thankful for.

—NORMAN VINCENT PEALE

Many traditions and mythologies contain teachings around the theme of descent and resurrection, sacrifice and rebirth. Each gift that we receive requires a sacrifice of some sort. Even the simplest meal has a cost: in time, money, and in the life of the plants or animals providing the ingredients. Today, let's journey about the sacrifices others have made on our behalf.

Journey

Journey to receive insight about (and give thanks for) the sacrifices that have been made on your behalf.

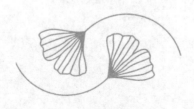

What Needs My Attention Today?

Never be so focused
on what you're looking for
that you overlook
the thing you actually find.

—ANN PATCHETT

With busy lives, it's easy to zoom past things that need our attention. Often these are external, like a roof in need of repair that you didn't notice until you sat outside and let your gaze wander. But sometimes they are internal. Internal things that need attention can be harder to pinpoint. For example, when you find yourself wanting to rebel against your usual routine by sleeping in, sitting still, or quitting your job, it may signal an underlying need for renewal, reflection, or change. Paying attention to these cycles can help us weather them productively and gracefully, rather than with fight and frustration. Let's pause to ask what needs attention today.

Journey

What needs my attention today?

Money

If more of us valued
food and cheer and song
above hoarded gold,
it would be a merrier world.

—J. R. R. Tolkien

What is your relationship with money? Adore it? Take it or leave it? Easy come, easy go? Rarely get to spend much time together? Do you think about it often, or is it just there when you need it? Regardless of the state of your relationship with money right now, let's ask for ways to improve it.

Journey

How can I improve my relationship with money?

Singing with Spirits

I believe in kindness.
Also in mischief.
Also in singing,
especially when singing
is not necessarily prescribed.

—MARY OLIVER

You've heard of choirs of angels, but what would it be like to sing with your own personal helping spirits? Let's try it today.

Journey

Journey to your helping spirits and sing.

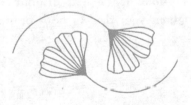

Appreciation

Let us rise up and be thankful,
for if we didn't learn a lot today,
at least we learned a little,
and if we didn't learn a little,
at least we didn't get sick,
and if we got sick,
at least we didn't die;
so, let us all be thankful.

—THE BUDDHA

Practicing gratitude is generally considered a good thing. Usually it involves coming up with a list of things for which we are grateful. What if we tried to hold appreciation as a mindset, rather than coming up with a list of specifics? Can inhabiting a state of appreciation shift the way we feel about our lives?

Journey

As much as possible, hold a state of gratitude and appreciation throughout your day, in both ordinary and non-ordinary reality.

What's the Rush?

*Time was rushing around me
like water around a big wet rock.
The only difference is,
I was not so durable as stones.
Very quickly I would be smoothed away.*

—LOUISE ERDRICH

I'm a fast walker. I find myself zipping around without realizing it because it is my typical speed; I'm often trying to get a lot of things done. When my daughter says, "Mom, please slow down!" I do of course, and it reminds me that my internal speed is often set to "high" unless I do something consciously to slow it down. Slower feels good, too. What is your default speed? If you find yourself moving quickly by default, maybe today would be a good day to see what it's like to move more slowly and deliberately.

Journey

Slow down intentionally today, in both your journey and in ordinary reality.

Empathic Overload

Man is a part of nature,
and his war against nature
is inevitably a war against himself.

—RACHEL CARSON

Are you empathic, drawing other's emotions and experiences into your body like a sponge? Most of us have been taught that empathy is a good thing, and it is . . . to a point. Understanding and having compassion for another person's suffering is good. This basic human ability helps us form meaningful bonds, steers us away from needlessly causing pain, and accounts, in part, for all sorts of beneficial impulses that keep society functioning with some level of decency. However, when we are deeply empathic and feel other's feelings as our own, we are easily burdened; it actually makes it harder to be of service. The energy of those emotions builds up like liquid in a sponge, and the accumulation can bring on symptoms that are immobilizing.

Journey

Ask for guidance about your level of empathic overload.

Healthy Compassion

*The measure of a country's greatness
is its ability to retain compassion
in time of crisis.*

—Thurgood Marshall

Compassion is a close counterpart to empathy, and it can help us avoid the sponge effect. Compassion allows us a healthy caring about others, without actually taking their energy into our own bodies. Healthy compassion is a result of developing good energetic boundaries. Immobilizing empathy is a result of porous energetic boundaries. Better boundaries can be learned. Both come generally from innate personality types and early life experiences.

Journey

Ask for guidance about having healthy compassion without taking other people's energy into your body.

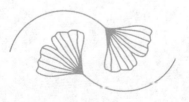

Healing with Nature

We must remember
how to honor and respect life
with each breath, step, word, and thought.
What you bless blesses you in return.
This is the power of reciprocity.

—Sandra Ingerman

Being in nature is one of my greatest joys, whether it's a long hike in the woods or simply sitting in the backyard watching the birds. Research has demonstrated that spending time in nature benefits our health in many ways, from regaining mental clarity to enhancing immune function. In addition to what the research finds, the natural world holds mysteries and beauty that are healing if we allow ourselves to wander.

Journey

How can I receive the most healing benefit from the natural world today?

Easing Burdens

People become attached to their burdens
sometimes more than the burdens
are attached to them.

—George Bernard Shaw

What would it feel like to let go of all your cares and worries? What if your pains and negative experiences lifted away? Today, let's ask for help in experiencing some carefree, easy moments.

Journey

Journey to experience yourself as pure spirit, free from any burdens.

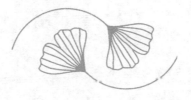

Party!

Spring is nature's way of saying,
"Let's party!"

—ROBIN WILLIAMS

If today were your birthday, what would be your ideal birthday party? Would you hang out alone and read a book, gather a few close friends and family, throw a huge bash? Or just chill with your favorite furry or feathered friends . . . oh wait, that's *my* idea of a fun party. Whichever combination you enjoy, throw yourself a party in non-ordinary reality today. And if possible, celebrate a little in ordinary reality, too.

Journey

Throw yourself a birthday party in non-ordinary reality.

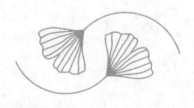

Feeling Powerful

Given the right circumstances
—being different is a superpower.

—Greta Thunberg

You've felt it: those moments when circumstances align and you feel your own strength, in big or small ways. Other times . . . not so much. Our sense of connection to our personal power waxes and wanes. We can all use an extra boost on occasion.

Journey

Journey and ask a helping spirit to remind you of your strength and power today.

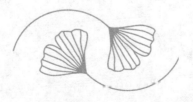

Kindness and Assumptions

*Children must be instructed
and trained to be kind.*

—Grandmother Tsering Dolma Gyaltong

When we make assumptions, it's easy to misinterpret people and situations. Being open to different interpretations of who people are, and what's happening under the surface at any given time, makes it easier to respond with kindness and compassion rather than judgment.

Journey

Journey for assistance in approaching people and situations with kindness and compassion.

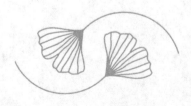

Your Body

If you dear little girls
would only learn what real beauty is,
and not pinch and starve
and bleach yourselves out so,
you'd save an immense deal of time
and money and pain.
A happy soul in a healthy body
makes the best sort of beauty
for man or woman.

—LOUISA MAY ALCOTT

With busy lives, it's easy to get disconnected from what our bodies are communicating to us. Subtle clues are often overlooked until more obvious signs like pain and illness emerge. Listening to your physical self on a regular basis helps give you valuable information about what your body needs to be healthy.

Journey

What does my body need today?

Animal Family

Lots of people talk to animals. . . .
Not very many listen, though. . . .
That's the problem.

—Benjamin Hoff

Pets are beloved members of the family. Is there anything we need to know about them today—their emotional state, how we relate to them, or their physical needs?

Journey

Please tell me anything I should know about my pets.

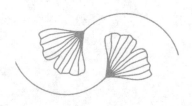

Next Steps

One must look at the next step
on the path ahead,
rather than the mountain in the distance,
or one would never reach one's goal.

—CASSANDRA CLARE

Let's ask this next question with no prelude and see what comes.

Journey

What are the next steps in my personal evolution?

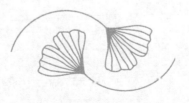

Being Prepared

By failing to prepare,
you are preparing to fail.

—Benjamin Franklin

In certain situations we know how to prepare; for example, how to pack for a trip, how to train for a race, how to study for an exam, or how to plan for a blizzard. Checklists are helpful for this kind of preparation. Other situations are less clear and therefore harder to anticipate; for example, when you aren't sure what situation is coming next. Today, we are asking for guidance about being generally prepared for what's upcoming, maybe in the next hour, day, or approaching weeks. What should you be aware of to effectively handle what life brings?

Journey

Please give me guidance about being prepared.

Unconditional Love

*Love has nothing to do with
what you are expecting to get—
only with what you are expecting to give—
which is everything.*

—KATHARINE HEPBURN

Throughout the year, we explore different ways of experiencing the energy of love. For today, think of someone or something that you love absolutely. It could be a person, a pet, a tree, or a favorite food, anyone or anything that you have simple (not conflicted) loving feelings toward.

Journey

Ask for help in experiencing pure unconditional love. What does it feel like?

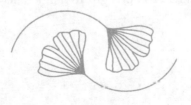

Giving Gifts

Giving gifts to others
is a fundamental activity,
as old as humanity itself.
Yet in the modern, complex world,
the particulars of gift-giving
can be extraordinarily challenging.

—Dr. Andrew Weil

Gifts are given for many occasions to a variety of people—those close to us and those we feel obliged to recognize. What gifts would be suitable to give to your helping spirits? These could mirror the kinds of gifts you give to the special people in your life whom you wish to honor, or they could be something radically different. Journey for guidance about what to give, and to whom, and then go ahead and give!

Journey

Journey for advice about a gift to honor a helping spirit.

Silence

Realizing fully
the true nature of place
is to talk its language
and hold its silence.

—Roshi Joan Halifax

It's hard to find silence in most places on the planet. What are the sounds around you? Find a way to experience silence (or as close to it as possible) today. What does it feel like?

Journey

Experience silence.

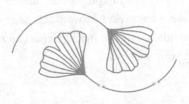

Snowy Landscapes

I wonder if the snow loves the trees and fields,
that it kisses them so gently?
And then it covers them up snug, you know,
with a white quilt;
and perhaps it says,
"Go to sleep, darlings,
till the summer comes again."

—LEWIS CARROLL

One of the beautiful aspects of shamanic journeying is that we can go to different landscapes. Whether traveling within the Middle World, or asking to be shown non-ordinary reality places, the possibilities for exploring are rich. Whether through journeying or the power of your imagination (or perhaps by looking out your own window), visit and explore a beautiful snowy landscape today.

Journey

Journey to a snowy landscape. What does it look like, feel like, sound like, smell like? How does your body respond to cold, to the quality of the light? Experience this environment with all your senses.

Cycles of Rest

Each day is a little life:
every waking and rising a little birth,
every fresh morning a little youth,
every going to rest and sleep
a little death.

—Arthur Schopenhauer

When the desire for rest comes at inconvenient or unusual times, we tend to resist it. But these can be the very times when our body needs it most, either because we are physically challenged and fighting to stay healthy, or because we need to prepare for the next phase. If we look to nature we will see that everything is cyclical and the rest phase is vital to the health of all systems, great and small. Birds put themselves to bed with the sun, flowers bloom for a period and then fall to the ground, and the seasons change consistently.

Journey

Journey and ask, "What does my body need to align my resting with natural cycles?"

New Heights

Any knowledge
that doesn't lead to new questions
quickly dies out:
it fails to maintain the temperature
required for sustaining life.

—Wisława Szymborska

The Upper World and Lower World in the spiritual realms are not a single level; there are many levels to each of those worlds. Ask to be shown a level of the Upper World that you haven't been to before.

Journey

Spirits, please show me a new level in the Upper World. Explore.

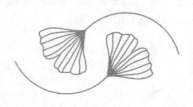

West

We call in and honor the spirits of the West:
Of adventure and strength
Of expansiveness and transformation.

—INVOCATION

Acknowledging the directions is part of indigenous cultures from around the world. Before starting ceremonies, and as a daily practice, we can honor the spirit of the directions and welcome them to be present. This can be done silently or with rattling or drumming by facing the direction and giving thanks.*

I was given the invocation above when I asked my helping spirits for guidance about creating my own ceremony for honoring the directions. What is your relationship with the West? Is there an energy or feeling associated with that direction for you? One way to honor West is with an afternoon greeting.

Journey

Journey to the spirits of the West to ask how you can honor and get to know them better.

---

* More information about honoring the directions is in the Appendix in "Invocation: Welcoming the Spirits and Directions."

Receiving Gifts

I'd rather risk an ugly surprise
than rely on things
I know I can do.

—HELEN FRANKENTHALER

Gifts can come in forms we don't expect, and sometimes are not entirely comfortable with. We often spend time wishing for things, when in reality we have a harder time truly receiving gifts that are presented to us. What divine gifts are in store for you today?

Journey

Journey and ask, "What divine gifts are available for me today?"

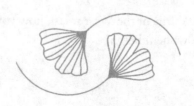

Ambiguity

Neurosis is the inability
to tolerate ambiguity.

—SIGMUND FREUD

Wouldn't life be easier if everything was black or white, yes or no, clear and easy to understand? Maybe. Wouldn't it also be boring, lacking nuance and subtlety, and maybe even cruel in its polarity? Living in the gray, in ambiguity and mist, can be confusing and exhausting. It has its rewards if we can navigate it with the sensitivity it calls for, tolerating its stubborn opacity, seeing the hazy shades that eventually coalesce into an elegantly formed picture.

Journey

If you have a situation in your life right now that is ambiguous, journey and ask a helping spirit how to navigate that *specific* situation gracefully and productively. If you don't have a specific situation, ask the same question, but for a *general* way to approach ambiguous situations gracefully and productively.

Mothers

It has been prophesized . . .
that the women will have the power
to move and to be leaders
and to bring people into the light.

—GRANDMOTHER FLORDEMAYO

The mother-child relationship is perhaps the most important one for setting our course in the world. Even before we are born, we establish that first bond with our mother. Whatever kind of relationship we have with our mothers (or with being a mother), it has given us something fundamental. Let's reflect on and recognize the importance of that relationship.

Journey

Honor and appreciate the mother-child relationships in your life. Ask to be shown any insights that are helpful for you today.

Celebrating Transitions

We must be willing
to get rid of the life we've planned,
so as to have the life that is awaiting us . . .
The old skin has to be shed
before the new one is to come.

—JOSEPH CAMPBELL

Some transitions, like births and deaths, are distinct, with clear rituals of celebration or grief. Other transitions are deeply significant to the individual experiencing them, but lack traditions that provide support from the community. These transitions can feel confusing and lonely. Divorce, the loss of a job or friendship, or the start of a new phase like adulthood or menopause, are times that we often try to muscle our way through. These periods are intense, but they would benefit from some deliberate attention. Are you going through any transitions right now? Are there any from the past that haven't received adequate time or attention to honor what you've gone through?

Journey

Journey for guidance about honoring a transition time in your life.

Writing for Healing

I wrote myself back together.
I wrote myself toward
a stronger version of myself.

—ROXANE GAY

Writing can be cathartic. The process of translating our thoughts and emotions into language and then separating those words from our internal space is powerful. In some instances it allows a release and a distancing from painful experiences. Sometimes it allows us to see things with new clarity that we missed when the experiences were confined to our internal world. Sometimes it's fun to just make things up. And of course, the choice to share what you write, or not, is yours. Might writing be a healing practice for you? Poetry, story, letters, journaling, stream of consciousness—in whatever form—consider using the written word in a healing way today.

Journey

Ask for guidance about writing as a healing practice.

Overwhelmed

I was a little excited but mostly blorft.
"Blorft" is an adjective I just made up
that means "completely overwhelmed
but proceeding as if everything is fine
and reacting to the stress
with the torpor of a possum."

—TINA FEY

Things do have a tendency to hit all at once. Many times I've said, "Can I please have one day when it's not *something*?" Plans get messed up, too many things happen (or fall apart) simultaneously for elegant solutions, minor things can feel like tragedies in the moment, and tragedies are more common than we care to admit. Over time I've tried to accept that the "somethings" can be pretty consistent; how we manage them makes all the difference. So breathe and find your tools for managing the overwhelm. Ask your guiding spirits to help you with advice about what to do and as backup in the moment. Call for help when you need it.

Journey

Journey to say, "Thank you for helping me manage when I'm overwhelmed." Any additional suggestions for handling that sensation are welcome.

Dedication and Discipline

We all have dreams.
But in order to make dreams come into reality,
it takes an awful lot of determination,
dedication, self-discipline,
and effort.

—JESSE OWENS

What are you dedicated to? What do you *want* to be dedicated to, and have a hard time finding the discipline to *do*? Let's ask for guidance in aligning the desire and the discipline today.

Journey

Please help me find the discipline to do the things that are important to me.

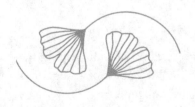

Mud Bath

The world is mud-luscious.

—E. E. CUMMINGS

A mud bath combines the benefits of all the elements: earth—obviously—as you are literally cradled in it; water, as water is added to make the mud a perfect consistency for you to be held and supported while still moving as you wish; fire, as the mud is heated to the perfect warmth for your comfort; and air, as you appreciate your breath while your head remains above the mud and the rest of you soaks in the minerals and warmth and goodness! Sound like fun? Let's try it today.

Journey

Journey and ask to be brought to a healing, soothing, rejuvenating mud bath.

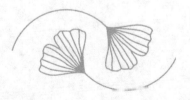

What Needs Seeing?

*In the jungle,
the Indian knows everything.*
—SURINAMESE PROVERB

When we ask to be shown what needs to be seen, we recognize that sometimes we don't know the most relevant questions to ask. Our perspectives are naturally limited, and so our requests can be, too. The helping spirits may be able to help us best by illuminating what is beyond our current vantage point.

Journey

On your journey today, ask, "Please show me what needs to be seen."

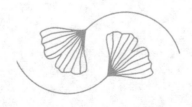

This Moment

The only time is Now.
All other times—past, present, and parallel—
can be accessed in this moment of Now,
and may be changed for the better.

—Robert Moss

While we do not have control over the passing of time, we have control over how mindful we are of our use of it. The value of keeping our awareness in the present is something that we often understand intellectually and have a harder time putting into practice. I work at it every day. I frequently stop to remind myself not to look forward or back, but to stay present in time, to look around me, love where I am and whom I'm with, and avoid worrying. Some days it works better than others. I encourage you to simply be in each moment of this day.

Journey

As much as possible, stay present in the moment today. Gently bring yourself back if you find yourself thinking too much about the past or the future. During your journey time, stay present in your body, in this place and time, in the Middle World. Paying attention to your breath moving in and out can help you focus.

Bones

*I have no history
but the length of my bones.*

—Robin Skelton

Your skeleton is the underpinning for your health. Your bones hold you upright, give you a foundation for movement, hold protective space for organs, and form strong scaffolding for muscles, tendons, and other soft tissue.

Journey

Journey to check in with your skeleton. What does your skeleton have to say today?

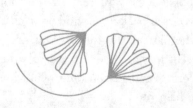

Practicing Kindness

*Doing a kindness produces
the single most reliable
momentary increase in well-being
of any exercise we have tested.*

—MARTIN SELIGMAN

Scientists and spiritual leaders agree on the power of kindness. The Dalai Lama famously said, "My religion is very simple. My religion is kindness." Kindness is the thread that weaves the fabric of a spiritually and emotionally whole life.

Journey

Where is kindness especially needed in my life today?

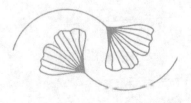

Plenty

There is enough in the world
for everyone to have plenty,
to live happily,
and to be at peace with his neighbors.

—Harry S. Truman

When do we have enough? Enough love, enough security, enough stuff, enough whatever we crave. Sometimes it's hard to tell, especially when we are used to being in seeking mode, or when the pursuit of one thing really masks a fear of the lack of something else. For today, let's act like we have enough to satisfy us on all levels.

Journey

Journey where you wish and repeat the mantra, "My life is plentiful."

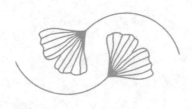

Blessing with Words

Words—so innocent and powerless as they are,
as standing in a dictionary,
how potent for good and evil they become
in the hands of one who knows
how to combine them.

—NATHANIEL HAWTHORNE

Words carry energy and emotion. Most of the major religions talk about words creating the world in the very beginning. Words have power, for blessing and for cursing. Today, let's ask for guidance about using words to uplift and combining our words with consciousness and kindness, creating blessings for those around us.

Journey

Please help me combine my words into blessings as I communicate with others.

True Nature

I'm a perfectly good carrot
that everyone is trying to turn into a rose.
As a carrot, I have good color
and a nice leafy top.
When I'm carved into a rose,
I turn brown and wither.

—MARY PIPHER

When you were born, you were encoded with a blueprint containing your true nature. As you lived and grew, that blueprint evolved. It was also affected, for better or worse, by the environment in which you lived, how your family treated you, the messages you received from peers, and the society around you. Today, ask for guidance about reconnecting with your true nature as it was before outside influences affected you. Who are you at your core?

Journey

Journey for insight into your true nature.

Receiving Love

Maybe love is like rain.
Sometimes gentle, sometimes torrential,
flooding, eroding, joyful, steady,
filling the earth,
collecting in underground springs.
When it rains,
when we love,
life grows.

—CAROL GILLIGAN

Being loving to yourself is as important as being loving toward others. You are enough, and you are lovable just as you are. If this is hard for you, you can start with something specific, even very small, about yourself. For instance, recognize and love your legs for moving you around as you wish, your fingertips for letting you feel your cat's silky fur, or your sense of humor for helping you laugh through hard times. In some way, send love to yourself today. If you are open to guidance around this topic, you can ask for that as well.

Journey

Journey to a helping spirit and ask them to guide you, perhaps showing you what it's like to be showered with love, and giving you practice at soaking it up. Then spend time within your journey offering love to yourself and taking it in.

Altar

The altar, as in prehistory,
is anywhere you kneel.

—Camille Paglia

We're familiar with creating sacred space in ordinary reality, sometimes with altars or shrines. We can also do this in non-ordinary reality, and those altars can be visited and tended in much the same way. The energy you put into them will be reflected back to you. Let's create an altar in non-ordinary reality that you can visit whenever you wish. Make it out of anything you hold dear, adorn it with flowers, icons, objects of nature, beautiful things that inspire you.

Journey.

Create an altar in non-ordinary reality.

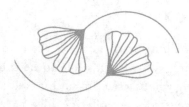

Indulgence and Abstinence

*Sometimes it is harder
to deprive oneself of a pain
than of a pleasure.*

—F. Scott Fitzgerald

It's really fun to indulge sometimes. And it's not a bad thing—within reason, of course. Abstaining also serves a purpose. Religious observances, such as Lent and Ramadan, encourage us to refrain from food, drink, or other things we enjoy. This helps develop discernment. Whether it's food or action or thought, the discipline to choose wisely is cultivated during these prescribed times of restraint. Could you use more abstinence or more indulgence in your life?

Journey

Journey for guidance about abstinence and indulgence.

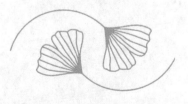

Being in Service

Service is a limitless opportunity;
it is the reason why we breathe.

—Michelle Obama

There are many ways to be of service. Sometimes we choose to serve by doing things we love and are naturally good at. Sometimes we have no choice and are called to serve by doing terribly hard things. We can always choose to thank those who have served on our behalf.

Journey

How can I best honor those who have served on my behalf?

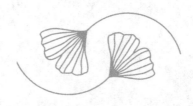

Spirits of the Land

Climb the mountains
and get their good tidings.
Nature's peace will flow into you
as sunshine flows into trees.
The winds will blow their own freshness into you,
and the storms their energy,
while cares will drop away from you
like the leaves of Autumn.

—JOHN MUIR

Have you ever been somewhere and felt the place had a particular quality or personality? Maybe it was loving, coolly appraising, playful, or complicated. Sometimes that tone comes from the spirits of the land itself. The land is ancient and is inhabited by spiritual beings. The land *is* a spiritual being! The more we live in harmony with the spirits of the land we inhabit, the better.

Journey

Journey to ask how to live harmoniously with the spirits of the land where you live.

Finding Joy in Difficult Times

How do we cultivate
the conditions for joy to expand?
We train in staying present.

—PEMA CHÖDRÖN

Cultivating joy is a process of looking inward rather than relying on external circumstances. Although many things can help us experience joy, it's really about maintaining an inward balance, even when life is complicated, even when it's painful. Ideally we find ways to spend our time, people to spend our time with, and places to spend our time in, that reflect our inner capacity to be joyful back to us, particularly in challenging times.

Journey

Journey to ask your helping spirits how to experience joy, even when circumstances are difficult.

Gifts of Interconnection

In the shamanic tradition
all life is both equal and sacred,
we are all interconnected,
and we are one with nature.

—CLAUDE PONCELET

Indigenous cultures operate under the basic premise that all beings are interconnected; nature is family. Animals and plants are included in that family, as are features of the land that Western societies typically consider inanimate, such as rivers, lakes, mountains, the sky, and the Earth itself. These are very different concepts of being, consciousness, agency, and relationship compared to Western thought. People from indigenous cultures generally do not place themselves above other beings, but within an integral, interdependent whole. Robin Wall Kimmerer, professor, author, and member of the Citizen Potawatomi Nation, explains, "It is understood that each living being has a particular role to play. Every being is endowed with certain gifts, its own intelligence, its own spirit, its own story. Our stories tell us that the Creator gave these to us, as original instructions. . . . These gifts are also responsibilities, a way of caring for each other." With this shared possession of uniqueness, and a role to play within a community, reciprocity is valued as the basis for health.

Journey

What is a unique gift I have to share with my community?

Power Symbol

Symbols give us our identity, our self image,
our way of explaining ourselves to ourselves
and to others.

Symbols in turn determine
the kinds of stories we tell,
and the stories we tell determine
the kind of history we make
and remake.

—Mary Robinson

Visual symbols concentrate power. They represent and condense complex ideas or processes and show them in ways that bypass logical thinking, going right to our intuitive understanding. Symbols of power have been used for ages by religious orders and organizations. We can have personal power symbols as well. Ask your helping spirits to give you a visual symbol to help you access your power (or something else that you choose) when you need it. Think of it as a way to quickly connect to something that is already yours, like a visual shortcut.

Journey

Journey for a personal power symbol.

Peace

If we want to see changes
first of all we need to be in peace inside ourselves,
and then we need to be patient
with the ones that have not yet arrived
in that place of peace.
—GRANDMOTHER MARGARET BEHAN

Peace can come from accepting what is, from resolving a situation that has been unsettled, and from simply letting yourself be without doing, saying, or expecting much. Whatever kind of peace you need today, try to give it to yourself. Ask your helping spirits for guidance if you need it.

Journey

Please help me find the peace I seek today.

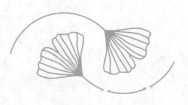

Body Scan: Upper

The body says
what words cannot.

—MARTHA GRAHAM

It would be ideal if we connected with our bodies each morning, taking time to listen to the incredible machine that allows us to literally *do* everything. Today we focus from the waist up, journeying inside your body. Intentionally scan from your head down to your waist; take as much time as you need with your head, face and neck, shoulders and arms, chest and back. Envision your organs and your skeleton. Sense your musculature and the soft tissue of your tendons and ligaments. How are things doing? What areas need your attention? This is a time for listening and perceiving with all your senses.

Journey

Journey to listen to your body from the waist up.

Body Scan: Lower

No one can listen to your body for you. . . .
To grow and heal,
you have to take responsibility
for listening to it yourself.

—JON KABAT-ZINN

Yesterday, we worked from the waist up. Today, journey inside your body from the waist down. Intentionally scan from your abdomen to your feet; take as much time as you need with your belly, backside and pelvis, thighs and knees, lower legs and feet. Envision your organs and your skeleton. Sense your musculature and the soft tissue of your tendons and ligaments. How are things doing? What areas need your attention? This is a time for listening and perceiving with all your senses.

Journey

Journey to listen to your body from the waist down.

Healing Art

Throughout the history of medicine,
including the shamanic healing traditions,
the Greek tradition of Asclepius,
Aristotle and Hippocrates,
and the folk and religious healers,
the imagination has been used
to diagnose disease.

—JEANNE ACHTERBERG

In its creation and in its appreciation, art can be an agent for healing. Whether you prefer the process of making art or looking at it, or even if you haven't felt connected to art in the past, let's journey for guidance about art's place in your healing today.

Journey

How can I bring healing art into my life today?

Pure Air

How sweet the morning air is! . . .
How small we feel
with our petty ambitions and strivings
in the presence of
the great elemental forces of Nature!
     —Sir Arthur Conan Doyle

Earth has been here for eons, and with it, the air in the atmosphere. How was the air different so long ago before human beings arrived and created cars and factories? What could we learn by experiencing that air? How might it surprise us? Ask your helping spirits to take you to a place with especially pure air.

Journey

Journey to a place and time from long ago with pure air.

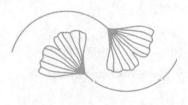

Restful Sounds

When anxious, uneasy
and bad thoughts come,
I go to the sea,
and the sea drowns them out
with its great wide sounds,
cleanses me with its noise,
and imposes a rhythm
upon everything in me
that is bewildered
and confused.

—Rainer Maria Rilke

What sounds are soothing to you? Some of my best summer nap memories are to the sounds of old window air conditioners because their white noise created such an insulating hum around the room. And then of course there is rain on the roof, and the brook outside the cabin in the woods. Pay attention to the sound environment that supports your rest today. Use your journey time to sink into sound or ask for guidance about how to use it.

Journey

Use sound to support your rest today.

Opportunities

*The shaman plunges into life
with mind and sense,
playing the role
of the cocreator.*

—SERGE KAHILI KING

Opportunities come at different times, in many forms, and with varying degrees of clarity. A promotion that involves moving to your dream city, where your new love interest happens to live? That's not one you're going to miss! Other opportunities are more subtle. We may not recognize them as such, and initially they might not even seem positive. There are also times that support personal action, and others where observation and contemplation are more important in order to *prepare* for when an opportunity arrives. What opportunities are available to you right now? How can you be best prepared for those coming in the near future?

Journey

Ask your helping spirits for advice about recognizing and taking full advantage of the opportunities that your life presents to you.

Night Sky

*We are made of
starstuff.*

—CARL SAGAN

Few experiences are more universal and primordial than contemplating the night sky. Friends of the ancient navigators, the stars help us orient ourselves in the larger geographic context. The vastness of an inky sky can also help us place ourselves in the larger context of existence.

Journey

Journey into a clear night sky, feeling the limitlessness of space. Then turn to look back upon the Earth. What insights come from this perspective? How does recognizing your (our) relative size affect your perspective and feelings about your self, your life, and your community?

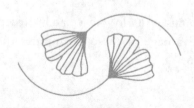

Emotional Health

A healthy woman is much like a wolf:
robust, chockful, strong life force,
life-giving, territorially aware,
inventive, loyal, roving.

—Clarissa Pinkola Estés

Our emotional state is like a lens through which we view the world. The proverbial rose-colored glasses can help the wearer stay optimistic, to see and experience situations in a positive light. If we are very sad, angry, or afraid, it's hard to have a genuinely positive life experience, even if the present moment is basically okay. On the flip side, if the emotions we have at a given time are affirming, even hard circumstances don't create as much negativity and turmoil. This doesn't mean we should be perky and upbeat all the time (unless that is your natural state, in which case, go for it!). Being healthy emotionally allows feelings to come and go while we stay fundamentally in balance.

Journey

Journey and ask, "How can I create greater emotional health?"

Giving Love

Love is what we are;
we don't get it from somebody,
we can't give it to anybody,
we can't fall in it
or fall out of it.
Love is our true Being.

—KRISHNA DAS

We are part of the web of life, a miraculous system that includes all living beings. Whatever you believe about the origins of life and the nature of the divine's role in the lives of all beings, sending love into that luminous web is a beautiful practice.

Journey

Send love to the web of life.

Something New

All my life through,
the new sights of Nature
made me rejoice like a child.

—MARIE CURIE

Have you ever explored just for the sake of exploring, without a destination? Or tried a new food or activity that was outside your scope of experience, or comfort? Trying new things stretches us to grow and expand. Having someone who is more practiced act as our guide allows us to explore in a safe way.

Journey

Journey to your helping spirits and ask, "Please show me something new."

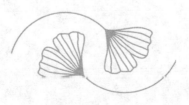

Who Needs My Kindness Today?

There can be no greater gift
than that of giving
one's time and energy
to help others
without expecting
anything in return.

—NELSON MANDELA

As we revisit kindness throughout the year, we look for guidance on the balance of giving and receiving. Today, we ask for clarity around being kind toward others.

Journey

Please show me if there is someone in my life who particularly needs kindness from me today.

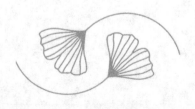

Fathers

It doesn't matter
who my father was;
it matters
who I remember he was.

—Anne Sexton

The father-child relationship is foundational and formative. Whatever kind of relationship we have with our fathers (or with being a father), it has given us something important. Let's reflect on and recognize the importance of that relationship.

Journey

Honor and appreciate the father-child relationships in your life. Ask to be shown any insights that are helpful for you today.

Physical Energy

Attention is psychic energy,
and like physical energy,
unless we allocate some part of it
to the task at hand,
no work gets done.

—MIHALY CSIKSZENTMIHALYI

Some of the things on our daily "to-do" list are vitally important to get done, while others are completely optional. Most things fall somewhere in the middle. Discernment around which things we focus on can help us stay balanced and healthy. Sometimes it's hard to know how to spend our daily allotment of physical energy.

Journey

On your journey ask your helping spirits, "Where should I focus my physical energy today?"

Back in Time to Love Yourself as a Child

It's children who are pure and truthful,
they are the ones who can come closest to God
because they are,
they're not conditioned to "seem like"
or to "appear to be,"
they are.

—Grandmother Clara Shinobu Iura

As children, some of our environments were filled with physical, emotional, intellectual, and spiritual nourishment, and others were not. Some of us were loved unconditionally, and others were neglected. Whatever the climate of your childhood, let's take a trip back in time today, and offer some warmth and support to your young self. Ask for guidance about what would be most helpful, or just think back to what you would have wanted at any given time (maybe a hug, words of encouragement, or simply time and attention) and give it to yourself today.

Journey

Journey and ask to be shown yourself as a child. Love yourself and offer what support is needed.

Healing Old Wounds

Wounds are the means through which
we enter the hearts of other people.
They are meant to teach us
to become compassionate
and wise.

—CAROLINE MYSS

Are there any wounds that you haven't resolved, healed from, or let go? When we let old wounds go untended, they can warp how we approach life. With a physical injury, the rest of the body compensates and eventually can get out of alignment. The same is true on an energetic and emotional level, as we shift and contort to protect those tender spots. It's not good for us in the long run. Now would be a good time to ask for some information and help.

Journey

Please help me heal from any old wounds I am still carrying, and show me any information that will help in my healing.

Honoring the Land

*An understanding of the natural world
and what's in it
is a source of
not only a great curiosity
but great fulfillment.*
— DAVID ATTENBOROUGH

The land we live on supports us physically and energetically. It has its own history and its own spirit. As part of creating a respectful and healthy relationship with the world around us, it's helpful to acknowledge how the land we live (work, play, love) on has served us, and to offer thanks in return.

Journey

Please show me a ritual I can do to honor the land I live on.

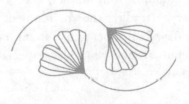

Reading the Environment

*The earth is real
and we are obliged
by the fact of our utter dependence on it
to listen more closely
to its messages.*

—William Ruckelshaus

Living shamanically involves interacting with your environment in ways that allow it to become a source of information and guidance. Interpreting signs in nature is possible by observing animals, plants, and elements, and their movements and interactions with you. In the man-made world, information of all kinds surrounds us. The timing and presentation of words, sounds, pictures, people, and conversations can all be part of how the environment is a source for relevant data and assistance.

Journey

Think of a question. In your journey, ask for help in divining an answer by reading the environment as you move through your day. Remember to pay attention to the movements and details around you today, especially in relation to your question.

Simplifying

Our life is frittered away by detail . . .
simplify, simplify.
—HENRY DAVID THOREAU

By paring away extraneous things, we can focus on what matters and enriches our lives. Whether it's saying no to optional activities that we don't really enjoy or giving away clothes that we no longer wear, we benefit by letting go of what's not enhancing our lives. Simplifying makes more time and space for what inspires us and what is truly important.

Journey

How can I simplify my life today?

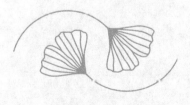

Power Song

The music for me is paradise.
I think it's where God lives.

—DIONNE WARWICK

Using sound and music to connect with the divine is part of most spiritual practices. Shamanic practice uses sound in many ways to shift states of consciousness. One way is by singing a personal power song given by the helping spirits. The song doesn't have to include words, and you don't have to be able to carry a tune. This is not about musical quality or talent; it's about a deeper connection. Just ask and see what comes.

Journey

Please give me a power song.

Honoring Spirit Teachers

A good teacher
teaches people how to see,
not what to see.

—RICHARD ROHR

In shamanism we spend a lot of time asking for help from compassionate spirits. It's nice to do something to honor them periodically, perhaps a gift of something they enjoy?

Journey

Journey to a helping spirit and ask, "What gift can I bring you?"

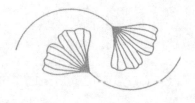

What Needs Hearing?

The main reason intuition is so important is this:
It is a clear sign that you are connecting
with your inner spiritual guidance system.
Intuition is a direct signal
from your deepest self
that you are navigating
from your true center.

—GAY HENDRICKS

What we ask is naturally bound to our awareness. When we ask to be told what we need to hear, we give the helping spirits permission to provide guidance beyond the scope of what we may conceive of asking them. This can be surprising and powerful.

Journey

Please tell me what I need to hear.

New Perspectives

We are like butterflies
who flutter for a day
and think it is forever.

—CARL SAGAN

Have you ever caught a glimpse of yourself in a mirror and seen yourself from an angle that felt unfamiliar? Or has someone described how they perceived you, and it was different from how you felt inside or thought you came across to others? These different viewpoints can be informative. We get used to experiencing ourselves from one perspective. Getting a fresh view can help us grow.

Journey

Please show me myself from a new perspective.

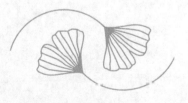

Facing Fears

When you are gripped by fear
in the face of an experience
that will take you beyond your comfort zone,
you may be at a point
of supreme opportunity.
You can either break down
or break through.

—Robert Moss

I've yet to meet someone who isn't afraid of something. Some people talk about their fears openly, while others bury them deep down. When we hide them, even from ourselves, they can grow, morph, and take up disproportionate space in our lives. Being clear on what our fears are can help us address them head-on. It also allows us to ask for help.

Journey

What am I afraid of? Please help me see my fears clearly.

Cool Water

I've known rivers ancient as the world
and older than the flow
of human blood in human veins.
My soul has grown deep
like the rivers.

—Langston Hughes

The elements are part of our bodies and our experience of being alive on the planet. Although it's not always possible to incorporate wild nature into our daily lives, we are surrounded by nature all the time, even in urban environments. We can also visit the natural world in our journeys whenever we choose. Today, let's experience water. Cool, clear, healing, soothing water.

Journey

Journey to experience yourself immersed in cool water, such as a clear running stream, a spring-fed lake, or the ocean.

North

We call in and honor the spirits of the North:
Of power and fortitude
Of deep rest and stillness.

—INVOCATION

Acknowledging the directions is part of indigenous cultures from around the world. Before starting ceremonies, and as a daily practice, we can honor the spirit of the directions and welcome them to be present. This can be done silently or with rattling or drumming by facing the direction and giving thanks.*

I was given the invocation above when I asked my helping spirits for guidance about creating my own ceremony for honoring the directions. What is your relationship with the North? Is there an energy or feeling associated with that direction for you? One way to honor North is with an evening greeting.

Journey

Journey to the spirits of the North to ask how you can honor and get to know them better.

---

* More information about honoring the directions is in the Appendix in "Invocation: Welcoming the Spirits and Directions."

Answers

You can tell whether a man is clever
by his answers.
You can tell whether a man is wise
by his questions.

—Naguib Mahfouz

Do you have a question (issue, problem, dilemma) that you've been mulling over for a while with seemingly no progress toward an answer? Today is the day to address it. Try to clear your mind of your past deliberations. Turn this question over to your helping spirits.

As you journey, try to be as open and receptive as possible to whatever you are shown, whatever you hear, whatever sensations you have in your body. When you return, write, record, draw, or in some way document it as thoroughly as possible *without* trying to come to a conclusion. Let it sit a while. Then come back and review and see what insights you have about your questions.

Journey

What is the answer to my question?

The Dynamics of Eating

After a good dinner
one can forgive anybody,
even one's own relations.

—Oscar Wilde

We frequently focus on *what* we eat. When we eat, how we eat, where we eat, and with whom we eat also impact how we nourish ourselves. For some, options are few, food may be scarce, and the time to prepare and eat meals may be limited; for others, options are plentiful. Let's ask about the dynamics of eating.

Journey

Are there aspects of the when, how, where, and with whom, of how I eat that need adjusting?

Planet Love

*Those who contemplate
the beauty of the earth
find reserves of strength
that will endure
as long as life lasts.*

—RACHEL CARSON

Today, let's think about the Earth, and specific places on the Earth, that we particularly adore and appreciate. In our journeys, let's go to them and surround them with love.

Journey

Journey to a place you love on the planet and express your love and appreciation.

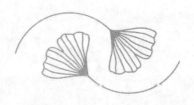

What Doesn't Belong?

In the process of letting go
you will lose many things
from the past,
but you will find yourself.

—DEEPAK CHOPRA

Is there something in your life right now that shouldn't be there? Are there steps you could take to remove whatever it is? You may know exactly what this is (have you been trying to get rid of it for years?) or you may be surprised by what comes up. Leave this question open for guidance. This could be a daily habit like a minor addiction to, say . . . chocolate (that's not mine at all), or it could be a macro-level energy like jealousy, for example.

Journey

Is there something that I need to purge? If so, please show me how to address it.

Limiting Beliefs

Developing inner values
is much like physical exercise.
The more we train our abilities,
the stronger they become.
The difference is that,
unlike the body,
when it comes to training the mind,
there is no limit to how far we can go.
—THE DALAI LAMA

Our thoughts help form what we believe is possible in our lives. Do you have any beliefs that hold you back from accomplishing what you are capable of?

Journey

Please help me identify any limiting beliefs I have now.

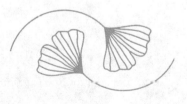

Fire and Ritual

Without the light,
no chance;
without the dark,
no dance.

—MARGARET ATWOOD

The element of fire can help transmute what does not serve us. Fire is also a common element in ceremony. Journey to the spirit of fire, and meet this powerful ally in transformation. Ask for a ritual or ceremony you can do to release and transmute any limiting beliefs you are holding now.

Journey

Journey to the spirit of fire and ask for a ritual to release limiting beliefs.

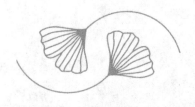

Internal Dialogue

The passageway
into the world of shamans opens up
after the warrior has learned
to shut off his internal dialogue.

—CARLOS CASTANEDA

Our internal dialogues can be harsh. We are often critical and unforgiving. Words are powerful. How we speak to ourselves internally affects our perceptions of ourselves and the world around us. Think about the effect you want to have and deliberately choose the words to use in your internal communication, and to what degree you want stillness or conversation.

Journey

Please give me a word (or words) to inspire me today.

Blind Spots

*Every age has its
massive moral blind spots.
We might not see them,
but our children will.*

—Bono

Most of us have blind spots, areas where we don't see as clearly as usual and are therefore vulnerable.

Journey

Please show me my blind spots. What can I do to be more aware of them in the future?

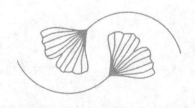

Lighten Up

Is it true that
cannibals don't eat clowns
because they taste funny?
—STEVEN WRIGHT

Have you been taking a situation or yourself too seriously? Where do you need to lighten up? As we explore the concepts of lightness and playfulness, let's get guidance around how you may have gone in the other direction.

Journey

Spirits, do I need to lighten up? If so, please show me about what. And how.

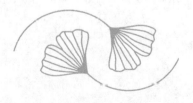

Rest and Temperature

It was one of those humid days
when the atmosphere gets confused.
Sitting on the porch,
you could feel it:
the air wishing it was water.

—JEFFREY EUGENIDES

What temperature is it where you are right now? Heat and humidity make it hard for a lot of people to feel energized and active; however, some people thrive in the heat. When it's cold, some of us turn inward and would rather curl up than go out. How does your body's energy level change with the seasons and the climate? Seasonal cycles of rest are important to think about and to honor.

Journey

Today, do one of the following: take a short power nap, ask for guidance around your ideal patterns of rest right now, or journey or meditate to simply be calm and relaxed.

Taking Action

*There is a vast difference
between positive thinking
and existential courage.*

—Barbara Ehrenreich

Knowing when to act is as important as knowing how to act. When we are grounded and feeling connected to our intuition, we can feel guided in our actions. Sometimes we feel at sea and uncertain. Today is about asking for guidance about the next step.

Journey

What should I take action on today?

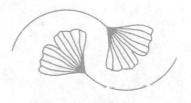

Kindness for Yourself

*Awakening self-compassion
is often the greatest challenge
people face on the spiritual path.*

—Tara Brach

As we revisit kindness throughout the year, we look for guidance on the balance of giving and receiving. Today, we ask for clarity around being kind toward ourselves.

Journey

Where should I be kinder to myself today?

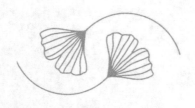

Why Me?

All spiritual blessings
you receive and create
are to be released
and given to others.
This way of passing it on
makes us transformers of spirit.
In this way
we are transformed.

—BRADFORD KEENEY

In shamanism, compassionate spirits are willing to partner with us through direct relationship. In all spiritual practices, there is a connection to the divine that is intended to help us. Are you interested to hear why your power animals and spirit teachers offered their assistance to you?

Journey

Ask a helping spirit why they have volunteered to work with you.

Appreciation

Rarely do we realize
that if we simply take time
to marvel at life's gifts
and give thanks for them,
we activate stunning opportunities
to increase their influence
in our lives.

—ANGELES ARRIEN

Throughout the year we explore gratitude and appreciation. For today, let's ask if there is something particularly relevant we have forgotten to be grateful for now.

Journey

What have I forgotten to appreciate about my life?

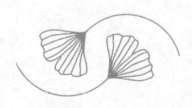

Time Crunch

Time limits are fictional.
Losing all sense of time
is actually the way to reality.
We use clocks and calendars
for convenience sake,
not because that kind of time is real.

—LESLIE MARMON SILKO

For many people from indigenous cultures, time doesn't exist in a linear fashion; it is more complex, with aspects of past, present, and future connected to each moment and to place. When we journey in the spiritual realms, we are moving outside of time as it's thought of from a Western viewpoint. Despite its seemingly orderly structure, the passing of time can feel quite variable. Sometimes it flies, sometimes it crawls. If your "to do" list is long, it can feel like there is never enough of it. Paying attention to your relationship with time can change how you perceive it.

Journey

Do I need to shift anything to be in a better relationship with time?

Dropping Form

The life of a man
is a circle from childhood to childhood,
and so it is in everything
where power moves.

—BLACK ELK

Most of us are very attached to our physical selves. We identify with our bodies, as well as our emotions and thoughts. What if we dropped those physical forms, and the mental and emotional aspects of being in the body, and experienced our purely spiritual selves periodically? For today, let's try stepping out of our bodies and simply being the light of our inner divinity.

Journey

Experience yourself stepping out of your physical body and being pure light.

Relationship Help

*Mutual caring relationships
require kindness and patience,
tolerance, optimism,
joy in the other's achievements,
confidence in oneself,
and the ability to give
without undue thought of gain.*

—FRED ROGERS

Is there a relationship that you are concerned about or would like some advice about? Today is the day.

Journey

Please give me some helpful information about my relationship with _____.

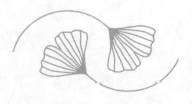

Your Sacred Space

Each place is the right place-—
the place where I now am
can be a sacred space.

—RAVI RAVINDRA

We can make just about any space sacred by what we bring
to it; however, places that are treated with reverence, used
for spiritual practices, and tended regularly help generate
an atmosphere of peaceful, healing energy. With whatever
space is available to you, create sacred space in your home.
A tabletop altar, a nook, a room, or an outside area can all
work.

Journey

Please give me guidance about creating sacred space in my
home.

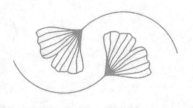

Provisions

My elders said,
"Know where your water comes from.
Know your fire.
Know where you are going
to find your food."
—Grandmother Mona Polacca

Most of us don't give much thought to the availability of supplies like flour, bread, cereal, and pasta; we simply go to the store and buy what we want. What if we had to plant, reap, mill, and bake everything we ate that was made from grain? Sounds exhausting to me. Let's pause to consider the efforts of other people that go into creating the things we enjoy. Pick whatever strikes you. Maybe it's the food you eat, or the car you drive, or the phone you use. Contemplate and appreciate the effort expended by others on your behalf.

Journey

I offer thanks to all the people who contributed to providing the bread I eat (car I drive, phone I use, etc.).

Younger Self

His older self
had taught his younger self a language
which the older self knew
because the younger self, after being taught,
grew up to be the older self and was,
therefore, capable of teaching.

—Robert A. Heinlein

If you could go back in time and offer words of advice or comfort to your younger self, would you? How might it have helped you, then and now? Let's do it today.

Journey

Pick a time in your life when you could have used guidance or love from your older, wiser self. Envision yourself providing that support to your younger self.

See Me

*Risk being seen
in all of your glory.*

—JIM CARREY

One of the benefits of working with compassionate helping spirits is that they see us with clarity and loving acceptance. They see our beauty and our flaws and accept the whole package. What would it be like to see ourselves with this kind of transparency, without getting caught up in self-doubt or vanity, fragile ego, or pride? Let's ask.

Journey

Spirits, please show me how you see me.

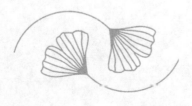

Happy Memories

*Gratitude is
when memory is stored in the heart
and not in the mind.*

—Lionel Hampton

Negative memories tend to fossilize in our thoughts. We fixate on them, replay them, and wonder what would happen if things went differently. We give negative memories a lot of power. Today, let's focus on a positive memory. Either choose one or ask for help with picking one, and let yourself sink into the sensations of a happy memory. Try not to get tangled in going forward or backward from that moment in time. Just enjoy the experience of that specific time and place.

Journey

Please help me to fully enjoy a happy memory.

Forgiving Someone

Self-love means
caring for ourselves enough
to forgive people in our past
so that the wounds can no longer damage us—
for our wounds
do not hurt the people who hurt us,
they hurt only us.

—CAROLINE MYSS

Where is the energy of forgiveness needed in your life today? Perhaps healing will come from forgiving someone from a past relationship, a family member or friend, a professional or institution that you feel has let you down, or even yourself. Leave it up to the helping spirits to guide you where to turn.

Journey

Journey for guidance about forgiveness.

Receiving Divine Love

If I were going to begin practicing
the presence of God for the first time today,
it would help to begin by admitting
the three most terrible truths of our existence:
that we are so ruined, and so loved,
and in charge of so little.

—ANNE LAMOTT

Open yourself to receiving love from divine energy today. Not because you are worthy or have done (or not done) anything in particular, simply because you are you.

Journey

Receive love from the divine. You can do this as a journey to a place you have particularly enjoyed in the Lower or Upper Worlds, or by staying still and allowing love to surround you. Ask for, and open yourself up to receiving, love from an aspect of the divine.

Larger Lessons

It was the possibility of darkness
that made the day seem so bright.

—Stephen King

Have you noticed that your life has themes, patterns of experiences that tend to repeat? These themes can give important clues to the lessons this lifetime has to offer. While it's not always fun, by looking carefully at the patterns you can often discern what needs to change to make it better. Sometimes the big patterns play out on a smaller scale on a daily basis.

Journey

What are the larger lessons I am here to learn in this life?

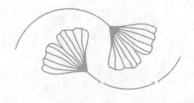

Social Service

*Think always to benefit others
and do no harm.*

—GRANDMOTHER TSERING DOLMA GYALTONG

We play different roles in the varying circles we move through: home, work, social, community. We're called to help in different ways; such as taking an active role, being a steadying presence, or even stepping back and letting someone else have the opportunity to step up. Today, we ask for guidance about your role in your social circles.

Journey

How can I best serve in my social circles today?

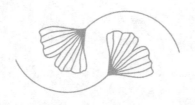

Crystals

In a crystal we have clear evidence
of the existence of a formative life principle,
and though we cannot understand
the life of a crystal,
it is nonetheless a living being.

—Nikola Tesla

Crystals are irresistible. They are beautiful, potent, and complex. Working with crystals for healing has a long history. It's important for us to become aware of what it means to work in responsible partnership with them. When crystals are brought to the mainstream market, they are mined from the earth. If you choose to work with crystals, try to be aware of where they are coming from and the impacts their extraction has on the earth and the people who are working to supply them. Today, let's connect with these exquisite beings and see if it's time to strengthen a relationship to one in particular.

Journey

Ask your helping spirits to take you to a crystal—perhaps in its natural state, or one you have already, or simply to give you some guidance about connecting with a crystal at this time for whatever is needed.

Healing from Loss

Grief is a natural emotion
which helps you to take care
of all the losses in life.
—Elisabeth Kübler Ross

Loss is part of life. Sometimes it's apparent how a loss makes way for something new. Other times a loss appears senseless and sad. Today, we are asking for help from the divine in healing from something you've lost.

Journey

Please help me heal and grow as I process my loss.

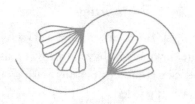

Celebration

Our time on this earth is sacred,
and we should celebrate every moment.

—PAULO COELHO

You don't need a special occasion to celebrate. Create your own party in non-ordinary reality today! Envision yourself in a favorite place, real or imagined, and create a celebration. It can be for just you or for whomever you'd like to be with you. It can have a specific purpose or it can simply be a party. Bring your favorite things—foods, drinks, decorations, music—or keep it very simple, whatever you like. Imagine yourself having a wonderful time!

Journey

Create a celebration (in non-ordinary reality).

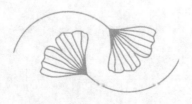

Stagnation

Contentment is not happiness.
Contentment is stagnation and decay,
whereas happiness is life and growth.

—Jiddu Krishnamurti

Have you ever had a stagnant period in your life? It might be with a specific aspect like work or a relationship, or it could be an overall sluggishness with everything you do or try. These periods can be frustrating. Sometimes it's best to wait them out with patience. There are also ways to potentially clear the blockages.

Journey

Please show me some ideas for moving through stagnant or sluggish periods of my life most effectively.

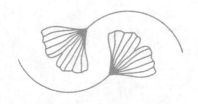

Open Guidance

The one seeking to demonstrate
the power of spiritual realization
in everyday affairs
should believe in Divine guidance . . .
and that everything in life
is controlled by love, harmony,
and peace.

—ERNEST HOLMES

Asking specific questions creates a clear intention and is powerful. Today, we balance structure and flow by leaving our question open.

Journey

What do I need to know today?

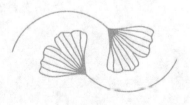

Disappointment

When you find your path,
you must not be afraid.
You need to have sufficient courage
to make mistakes.
Disappointment, defeat, and despair
are the tools God uses
to show us the way.

—PAULO COELHO

We all face disappointment. After some time has passed, sometimes we can see that there was a benefit received from the experience even though it was not apparent at the time.

Journey

Please show me how a disappointing experience served me in some way.

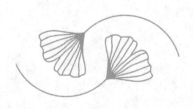

Power of Words

The power of words
told over generations,
remembered from trees,
dreams and ancestors,
is a power inherent in indigenous cultures,
contained within the fabric
of our way of life.

—Winona LaDuke

Do you find yourself saying things you wish you could take back? Do you tend to stay quiet even when you have something to say? Do you overshare? Words have power. Choosing which ones to use, how many to use, and when to use them is important.

Journey

Please give me guidance around my verbal communication today.

301

Kindness

You can always give something,
even if it is only kindness.

—ANNE FRANK

Being kind applies to how we treat individuals, and it can also relate to how we handle circumstances in general. Approaching complex interactions with kindness (hopefully avoiding both pity and judgment) we can sometimes shift the tone of challenging relationships and situations.

Journey

Are there any situations that particularly call for kindness today?

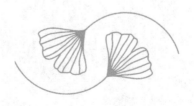

Strong Energy Boundaries

What you don't resist
persists like hell
and spreads all over the place.

—STARHAWK

Having a strong energetic body and the ability to discern and maintain energetic boundaries helps to foster good mental and physical health.

Journey

Please help me keep my energy body strong and give me any information I need about my energetic boundaries today.

Insect Eyes

Ants are fundamentally alien to us in many ways,
but they are always coming up with solutions
to problems that are familiar to us,
like traffic jams, public health,
food scarcity, and so forth.

—Mark Leviton

One way to perceive the world with expanded senses and to process information in new ways is to see from perspectives outside our usual vantage point. It can also help us live more harmoniously with other beings and learn something about ourselves. In this journey, prepare for a really different vantage point!

Journey

Journey to experience the world from an insect's point of view.

Intuitive Connection

Every time you don't follow your inner guidance,
you feel a loss of energy,
loss of power,
a sense of spiritual deadness.

—Shakti Gawain

Regularly working out your intuitive muscles helps them grow. Time spent in silence ready to *receive* information is a great way to increase the likelihood that you will hear when your intuition has something to say. Today, we are asking for guidance about your intuitive connection and ways to foster it.

Journey

Please give me guidance about strengthening my intuitive connection.

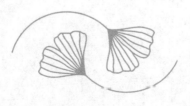

Patience

Patience is the companion
of wisdom.

—Saint Augustine

Is it possible to be too patient? In general, patience is a positive thing. In today's journey we are seeking guidance on how to cultivate patience—for ourselves, others, situations—but also to have discernment around when action rather than forbearance is most appropriate.

Journey

Please give me guidance around cultivating appropriate patience.

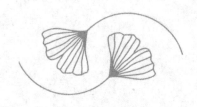

Confidence

We do not need magic
to transform our world.
We carry all of the power we need
inside ourselves already.

—J. K. ROWLING

Having confidence and self-assurance helps wherever you are and whatever you are doing. Today, let's create a ritual or ceremony that helps increase confidence.

Journey

Please show me a ritual I can do to increase my self-confidence.

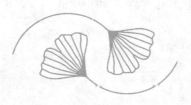

Turn It Over

Spiritual teachings
do not come so much
from the lips of a teacher
as they come from an intuitive sympathy
with the right teachers,
the most important being God,
whose voice may speak
through nature.

—JAMES SWAN

Have you ever felt the relief of turning a project that's been weighing on you over to someone else? While we can't abdicate personal responsibility, it can be helpful to take a break and to turn a problem over to the divine for a while. Surprising things can happen when we step out of the way!

Journey

Journey to a helping spirit or aspect of the divine and ask them to help you with a situation. Turn it over and say thank you.

Passion

Our passions,
when well exercised,
have wisdom;
they guide our thinking,
our values,
our survival.

—DANIEL GOLEMAN

What do you feel passionate about? What excites or inspires you? Are there activities where you lose track of time, or feel truly joyful? Where do you find meaning? These may be relatively easy to answer or you may come up blank. Either way is okay. Today, you are asking to reconnect with what inspires your passion, either for some help identifying it or practical ways to get more of it in your life.

Journey

Please help me (re)connect with passion.

What Is Not Mine?

The most potent weapon of the oppressor
is the mind of the oppressed.

—STEVEN BIKO

Are you holding anything that is not yours? Worries, responsibilities, energy in your body, trauma, ancestral experiences—anything that is not natively yours that it's time to let go of.

Journey

Please help me identify anything I am holding that is not mine.

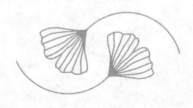

Removing What Is Not Mine

The art is not one of forgetting
but letting go.

—Rebecca Solnit

Yesterday you asked for help identifying what you are holding that is not yours. Today, you are going to ask for help in letting it go. You may have a direct healing or be given guidance or even a ritual to do later.

Journey

Please help me be free of what is not mine.

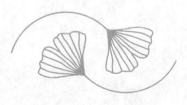

Practical Love

Love is everything it's cracked up to be ...
It really is worth fighting for,
being brave for,
risking everything for.
And the trouble is,
if you don't risk anything,
you risk even more.

—ERICA JONG

Today is a day for giving love. Where you send your love today is up to you.

Journey

Be loving today. Practically, while you are going about your day, and also within your journey, focus on giving love.

Your Body

*The moment you change your perception
is the moment you rewrite
the chemistry of your body.*

—DR. BRUCE H. LIPTON

With busy lives, it's easy to get disconnected from what our bodies are communicating to us. Subtle clues are often overlooked until more obvious signs like pain and illness emerge. Listening to your physical self on a regular basis helps give you valuable information about what your body needs to be healthy.

Journey

What does my body need today?

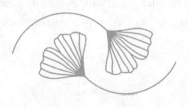

Signs and Omens

Nobody sees a flower really;
it is so small.
We haven't time,
and to see takes time—
like to have a friend takes time.

—GEORGIA O'KEEFFE

Have you ever had an unusual encounter in nature? Did it feel like a random event or something more personal? When we pay attention, these anomalous encounters tend to happen more frequently. Part of seeing with shaman's eyes is to become attuned to the elements, animals, and plants, both in their interactions with each other and in their interactions with us. By becoming attuned like this, we can develop the ability to interpret the signs in the natural world. For this journey we ask for insight into an experience you had that felt like a sign or omen.

Journey

Remember a distinct encounter you had in nature. Ask one of your helping spirits for insight into the occurrence.

Ancient Land

Humans are new here.
Above us, the galaxies dance out toward infinity.
Under our feet is ancient earth.

—John O'Donohue

The land has been here for millions of years. We are new-comers. What was it like before we arrived? What might we learn from the ancient land itself, or simply from looking at the land we live on today as it looked ages ago? Ask your helping spirits to give you a glimpse of this ancient land.

Journey

Journey to the ancient land and explore. Bring a helping spirit with you.

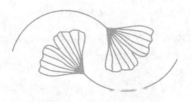

Sky/Above

We call in and honor
the spirits of the heavens (or sky):
The celestial beings and divine guidance
The canopy that protects and embraces us.

—INVOCATION

Acknowledging the directions is part of indigenous cultures from around the world. Before starting ceremonies, and as a daily practice, we can honor the spirit of the directions and welcome them to be present. This can be done silently or with rattling or drumming by facing the direction and giving thanks.*

I was given the invocation above when I asked my helping spirits for guidance about creating my own ceremony for honoring the directions. What is your relationship with the Sky? Is there an energy or feeling associated with that direction for you? One way to honor the heavens is with a bedtime prayer of gratitude.

Journey

Journey to the spirits of the heavens to ask how you can honor and get to know them better.

---

* More information about honoring the directions is in the Appendix in "Invocation: Welcoming the Spirits and Directions."

Inner Critic

I just look at women sometimes
and I just want to ask them,
"Do you know
how fabulous you are?"

—Viola Davis

Are you your harshest critic? Today, ask for guidance (if you need it) about areas in which you are overly critical to and about yourself. In your thoughts, words, and deeds today, make an effort to be kinder, and less critical. In your journey, ask your helping spirits to assist you in this process.

Journey

Journey and ask for help being less critical of yourself.

Disintegration

Sometimes good things
fall apart
so better things can
fall together.

—Marilyn Monroe

Have you ever felt like your life was disintegrating? Or maybe pieces of it were falling off? In shamanism we talk about dismemberment, an experience when you are torn apart on a spiritual level. The experience itself can be unpleasant. Do you avoid even necessary pain at all costs, or do you face it and move through it? Do you treat yourself gently or harshly? Are you able to keep relatively centered or do you find yourself wildly off course? These are times of powerful initiation. How you handle them makes a big difference.

Journey

Please give me some ways to stay healthy during times of disintegration.

Dolphin

To the Dolphin alone,
beyond all other,
nature has granted
what the best philosophers seek:
friendship
for no advantage.

—PLUTARCH

Brilliant, sleek, playful, dolphins have fascinated humans for ages. Cultures around the world have stories of human/dolphin interaction and different ways of honoring our dolphin brothers and sisters. One classical tale describes Apollo taking the form of a dolphin as he was searching for the place to establish his temple. We know his sacred place as the Temple at Delphi, perhaps related to *delphis,* Greek for dolphin. For many people of Australia and New Zealand, dolphins are sacred. Humans and dolphins fished cooperatively, and dolphins would be consulted on "important tribal matters," sometimes through telepathy.

You may or may not have dolphin as a helping spirit, but perhaps if you ask, a dolphin will help you with some advice, or will share some of its wisdom and power with you.

Journey

Ask to meet a dolphin spirit and share some of its wisdom and power.

Another Culture

The world in which you were born
is just one model of reality.
Other cultures
are not failed attempts at being you;
they are unique manifestations
of the human spirit.

—WADE DAVIS

We gain wisdom from understanding different perspectives. What would it be like if you were from another culture? Which opinions of yours might stay the same and which might change? How would you experience the world differently? How might people treat you differently? We can never really know, but we can ask to be given some insight. In this journey, you can pick a specific culture or leave it up to the spirits to choose for you.

Journey

Please show me what it would be like to be from a culture other than my own.

Peace

The most powerful tool with us
is to pray and pray with other communities
for world peace.

—GRANDMOTHER BEATRICE
LONG VISITOR HOLY DANCE

Seeking inner peace is an aspect of most spiritual practices. Doing so in a chaotic and conflicted environment makes the process more difficult. The collective global consciousness is affected by the inner states of billions of people. If your goal is peace, what can you do to create it, in your inner world and in the world around you? Sometimes seemingly small gestures have a remarkable ripple effect. Try not to be discouraged or to carry the weight of the world on your shoulders.

Journey

How can I contribute to peace in the world, and within myself, today?

Back in Time
to Love Yourself as a Teen

I want her,
really bad,
to know she is enough.

—ALICIA KEYS

Our teenage years can be among the most difficult. The meta-morphosis from child to adult is excruciating, and sometimes hard to be around. Even the most well-intentioned adult sometimes struggles to provide the best love and support to a teen. It can be a precarious time. What would you like to say to yourself as a teenager from the vantage point of your adult self? What do you think your teenage self most needed to hear? Most importantly, send your teenage self love.

Journey

Journey and ask to be shown yourself as a teenager. Love yourself and offer what support you would have wished to receive at that time.

Emotional Energy

Don't ask what the world needs.
Ask what makes you come alive,
and go do it.
Because what the world needs
is people who have come alive.

—HOWARD THURMAN

Emotional energy is as important to manage as physical energy. When something (or someone) drains us emotionally, it's often much harder to find the physical energy to get things done. On the flip side, when we do things that uplift us emotionally, time can fly by, and we can feel more energized even after working. Being aware of what feeds you and what drains you emotionally can help you discern how to manage your emotional energy.

Journey

Where should I focus my emotional energy today?

Discipline

Talent is cheaper than table salt.
What separates the talented individual
from the successful one
is a lot of hard work.

—STEPHEN KING

Having the discipline to complete a long-term project or stick with a daily practice is valuable. Discipline that overrides pressing emotional or physical needs pushes past the point when it's healthy. Most of us could probably use a little more discipline somewhere in our lives. Today is about getting help around this topic.

Journey

Please help me discern how to be disciplined for my highest good today and in general.

Play with a Helping Spirit

*Animists are people
who recognize that the world
is full of persons,
only some of whom
are human.*

—Graham Harvey

One of your power animals or teachers wants to play with you today. I wonder what you'll be doing!

Journey

Journey to play with a helping spirit.

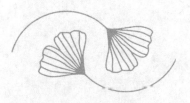

Rest from Work

Almost everything will work again
if you unplug it for a few minutes,
including you.

—ANNE LAMOTT

Whether the work you do is paid or not, in or out of the home, take time today to honor the work you do—and to take a break from it if possible. During your journey time today, shift from your working state of mind and let yourself do whatever you want, as long as it is not work. Even a spiritual practice that generally uplifts and inspires us can begin to feel like work if we don't allow ourselves enough freedom and rest.

Journey

Take a day off from formal spiritual practice.

Deeper Kindness

I've learned that
people will forget what you said,
people will forget what you did,
but people will never forget
how you made them feel.

—Maya Angelou

Kindness is not always soft and gentle. There are many ways to be kind. Some kindnesses are overt, others subtle. Some are met with positive responses at the time, while some are not appreciated in the moment but are over time. Some truly kind gestures are never recognized for what they are and are difficult for both the giver and receiver. How do you define kindness in theory and practice?

Journey

Journey to ask your helping spirits for advice about taking kindness to a deeper level.

New Levels

The shamanic ladder
is the earliest version of the idea
of an axis of the world,
which connects the different levels of the cosmos,
and is found in numerous creation myths
in the form of a tree.

—JEREMY NARBY

In shamanic journeying we often venture into the Upper or Lower Worlds. Each of those worlds has levels. Just as in our ordinary-reality lives, we have places that we return to repeatedly and places we visit that are new. Today, ask your helping spirits to show you a level in the Lower World that you haven't visited before.

Journey

Spirits, please show me a new level in the Lower World. Explore.

Nourishing Relationships

Today, we turn to one person
to provide what an entire village once did:
a sense of grounding, meaning, and continuity. . . .
Is it any wonder that so many relationships
crumble under the weight of it all?

—ESTHER PEREL

Just as with our relationships in ordinary reality, our relationships with helping spirits benefit from some tending. Since we can have many relationships in our lives, with people and with helping spirits, it's good to make time to nourish those relationships. Today, pick a helping spirit that perhaps you haven't connected with in a while and simply spend time together.

Journey

Journey to a helping spirit and enjoy being together.

Love Balm

Can one invent verbs?
I want to tell you one:
I sky you,
so my wings extend so large
to love you without measure.

—FRIDA KAHLO

What would you like to receive love for today? Perhaps a balm for a suffering heart, a disappointment, or a physical or emotional wound?

Journey

Ask your helping spirits to give you love for whatever you choose today.

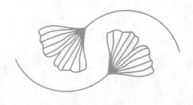

Vulnerabilities

We need to learn
to soothe ourselves
so we're not making our happiness
dependent upon someone else.

—LISSA RANKIN

Vulnerability isn't a bad thing. A certain level of vulnerability allows intimacy. However, vulnerabilities you're not aware of can sabotage you, causing a loss of personal power. If you are vulnerable energetically and are leaking power, it's helpful to understand how and take steps to correct it.

Journey

Please show me any areas in my life where I am vulnerable in an unhealthy way.

Ceremony for Boosting Power

*The Toltecs believe
that everyone is a nagual,
but the shamans
are the ones whose eyes
are open to this realization.*

—Don Miguel Ruiz

Yesterday we journeyed to ask if there were any areas of vulnerability or personal power loss that needed to be addressed. Today we ask for a ritual or ceremony we can do to help boost our personal power and strengthen those areas.

Journey

Please show me a ritual I can do to heal and boost my personal power.

What Needs Seeing?

Listen, wait, and be patient.
Every shaman knows
you have to deal with the fire
that's in your audience's eye.

—KEN KESEY

When we ask to be shown what needs to be seen, we recognize that sometimes we don't know the most relevant questions to ask. Our perspectives are naturally limited, and so our requests can be, too. The helping spirits may be able to help us best by illuminating what is beyond our current vantage point.

Journey

Please show me what needs to be seen.

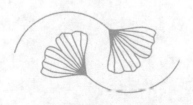

Gratitude of the Spirits

The deepest principle
in human nature
is the craving to be appreciated.

—WILLIAM JAMES

Do you think your helping spirits are grateful to you in any way? Let's ask.

Journey

Are there any ways that my helping spirits are grateful for me?

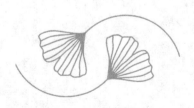

Tree Power

Trees are sanctuaries.
Whoever knows
how to speak to them,
whoever knows
how to listen to them,
can learn the truth.

—HERMANN HESSE

In a world, and a time, that often feels chaotic and over-whelming, one of the best ways to settle your body and mind is by grounding. One of the most effective (and enjoyable) ways to ground is with the help of the strong, solid energy of trees. If you can get outside today and sit against a tree, that's great. If not, experience yourself as one. It's one of my favorite practices. Feel your trunk holding you upright and solid. Feel your roots going deep into the ground, anchoring you, helping you withstand any wind. Feel your branches reaching high into the cool blue sky giving you new per-spective and fresh air.

Journey

Visit a tree and ask if you can share its energy. Envision yourself merged with the tree.

Setting Things Right

*The journey to happiness
involves finding the courage
to go down into ourselves
and take responsibility
for what's there:
all of it.*

—RICHARD ROHR

The Jewish holiday Yom Kippur is a day of atonement. It embodies an important concept, making time to review one's sins and ask for forgiveness. We can do this at any point in the year whether or not we practice Judaism. I like the idea of doing a periodic review to see if there is anything I need to set right. By "like" I mean I think it's a good idea, not that it's a pleasurable process. If there is something I can say or do to make up for my mistakes, I'd rather do it now and get it over with.

Journey

Journey to ask, "Is there anything that needs setting right today?" And if so, what would be the best way to do it?

Clearing Space

Don't own so much clutter
that you will be relieved
to see your house catch fire.

—WENDELL BERRY

Most of us make some effort to keep our home and work-space physically clean. I know there is a lot of variation here! Keeping your spaces clear energetically is a good idea, too. Whether through sacred sounds (chimes) or smells (incense), spaces have historically been tended energetically. Perhaps you may be given some new ways today.

Journey

Please show me some ways to clear my space energetically.

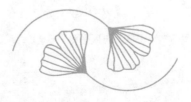

Dancing

*Dance is
the movement of the universe
concentrated in an individual.*

—Isadora Duncan

Like many things that involve deep self-expression, people have wildly different reactions to dancing. For some, sinking into the movements of the body is a relief and release from the confines of tension and thought. For others, the thought of dancing in public is a nightmare. Sometimes it depends on the kind of dancing. One way to explore the beauty of this form of expression without the added pressure of an audience, and with the added delight of a perfect partner, is to dance with a helping spirit. You can also do this as a solo dance if you prefer. Let yourself enjoy the movement of your "body" free from any physical or emotional restraints that you have in ordinary reality. Any kind of music (or silence), any environment, just enjoy moving.

Journey

Journey to dance with a helping spirit.

Creation

Science without religion
is lame.
Religion without science
is blind.

—Albert Einstein

What do you believe about the creation of humans, animals, plants, and the Earth itself? Each religion has its own creation story, as does science. As individuals we often have some variations on the idea of creation and what it means to us personally. Today, let's reflect on that and ask for some guidance about our own personal creation story.

Journey

Journey for insight about creation.

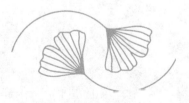

Animal Blessings

Until one has loved an animal,
a part of one's soul
remains unawakened.

—ANATOLE FRANCE

One of my favorite daily rituals is to meditate with my animals. (I call it "petitation," but discovered that someone else actually claims a trademark on this term!) We all look forward to it. If I don't get myself ready to sit fast enough, one of my cats will paw at my legs and meow until I get settled. It's our time to give and receive love from one another. Are there any creatures (tame or wild) in your life who could use a little love and attention today?

Journey

Honor the animals in your life. Shower them with love and attention.

Turning the Tables

I am still making order
out of chaos
by reinvention.

—JOHN LE CARRÉ

There are times when it's helpful to take on roles that are unfamiliar to us. For example, if you are usually a caretaker, allowing yourself to be cared for, or if you are usually the planner, being the more spontaneous partner. Sometimes these role reversals happen over the course of time without intention or forethought, as when adult children need to start caring for aging parents. We can also stretch ourselves to evolve into more balanced beings by welcoming experiences that turn the tables, allowing us to practice some other ways of being. This can be fun and enlightening.

Journey

Are there places in my life where I would benefit from turning the tables and playing a different role?

Foods to Avoid

*Don't eat anything
your great-grandmother
wouldn't recognize as food.*

—MICHAEL POLLAN

We have to eat. What, when, how, where, and with whom we do it involves a lot of choices. The foods we eat affect our bodies profoundly, and the concept of nourishing eating and eating habits is complicated. It's helpful to check in periodically for guidance around food and eating.

Journey

Are there foods I should avoid to keep my body healthy today?

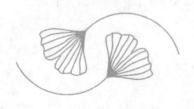

Feeling Supported

I was once afraid of people saying,
"Who does she think she is?"
Now I have the courage to stand and say,
"This is who I am."

—OPRAH WINFREY

Whether the support is spiritual, practical, or personal, sometimes we just don't feel it. It doesn't mean it isn't there, but sometimes we need a little help to see it; invisible ink needs a black light or a magic revealing spell to be seen. Sometimes it's simple but not obvious.

Journey

Please help me see the support that is available to me.

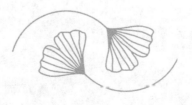

Honoring Those Who Came Before

We all share ancestors,
because humanity is humanity.

—BERNADETTE REBIENOT

Many generations have come before us; some lived on the specific land you live on now, others came from different places. We may share genes, memories, or intersections in time and space, and we all share the experience of being human, weaving a thread through history. Let's honor those who came before us. Choose someone specific whom you know, or, in a more general way, honor the people who lived on your land long ago, or your ancestors who came from somewhere else.

Journey

Journey to honor those who came before you.

Forgiving Yourself

You must learn to forgive yourself. . . .
And then take a further step
and use all that energy
that you used in condemning yourself
for improving yourself.

—Peace Pilgrim

Even generally forgiving people can have a hard time forgiving themselves. Is there anything that you should let go of and forgive yourself for?

Journey

Is there anything I need to forgive myself for today? Please show me a ritual to help me forgive myself.

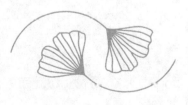

Soothing Care

The most valuable thing
we can do for the psyche, occasionally,
is to let it rest, wander,
live in the changing light of room,
not try to be or do
anything whatever.

—MAY SARTON

Any highly functioning machine needs to be well cared for. I mean no disrespect in calling us machines; sometimes it helps to look at ourselves a little dispassionately. Some people confuse self-care with selfishness. If you want to run well, you need to take care of yourself. One way to receive care is on the spiritual level. Ask for soothing, nurturing care from your helping spirits. This can be incredibly restorative.

Journey

Journey to a helping spirit to receive divine care.

Remembering

What matters in life
is not what happens to you
but what you remember
and how you remember it.

—Gabriel García Márquez

As we get older and fall into routines of work and relationships, we can forget aspects of ourselves that are valuable, like qualities, abilities, or interests. There also may be talents or potentials waiting to be discovered that we never knew we had. Let's explore this today.

Journey

Journey to a helping spirit and ask, "Is there something about myself that I need to be reminded of today?"

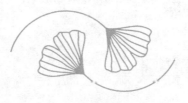

Clearing Emotions

Emotional self-awareness
is the building block
of the next fundamental
emotional intelligence:
being able to shake off
a bad mood.

—DANIEL GOLEMAN

Has your judgment ever been clouded by anger? Have you been too sad to think straight or make good choices? Having emotions is part of being human; however, we have choice about how we handle them. Ideally, we can experience emotions without allowing difficult ones to move in for the long term. Let's ask for some ways to help transform or transmute those emotions that trouble us and don't serve us.

Journey

Please show me a method to transmute troubling emotions.

Your Effect on Others

The heart was viewed as a place
where a being
is in constant communication
with "all that is."

—Ilarion Merculieff

We can never get a truly objective perspective on how we affect others, but wouldn't it be helpful to know? Perhaps our helping spirits can give some insight into whether we are having the impact that we think. Of course this likely varies from person to person, so you can ask in general or about a specific person.

Journey

How do I affect others?

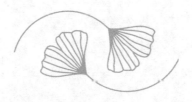

Love for the Divine

Our hearts irrigate the earth.
We are fields before each other.
How can we live in harmony?
First we need to know
We are all madly in love
With the same God.

—St. Thomas Aquinas

Today, let's focus our love on the manifestations of the divine that we feel connected to. This can be a specific embodiment, like Jesus, the Buddha, or a personal helping spirit; more of a universal divinity, like God or Spirit; or any other way that you experience the sacred.

Journey

Honor and send love to the divine today.

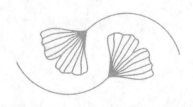

Air and Breath

Our most basic common link
is that we all inhabit this planet.
We all breathe the same air.
We all cherish our children's future.
And we are all mortal.

—John F. Kennedy

Is there an über element? If so, air has got to be it. Unseen, understated, perhaps underappreciated, air is a must-have. Where I live, in the northern hemisphere in a region of deciduous trees, air and the falling leaves have fascinating interactions, especially in the fall. The leaves move in varied ways, singly twirling down slowly and gracefully, or en masse sideways in a burst; really it's the air that animates and breathes movement into them. Air animates us, too, each moment with our breath. How can you interact with air more productively, joyfully, healthily?

Journey

Journey and ask how you can interact with air (and your breathing) more productively, joyfully, and healthily.

Answers

Follow your inner moonlight;
don't hide the madness.

—ALLEN GINSBERG

Do you have a question (issue, problem, dilemma) that you've been mulling over for a while with seemingly no progress toward an answer? Today is the day to address it. Try to clear your mind of your past deliberations. Turn this question over to your helping spirits.

As you journey, try to be as open and receptive as possible to whatever you are shown, whatever you hear, whatever sensations you have in your body. When you return, write, record, draw, or in some way document it as thoroughly as possible *without* trying to come to a conclusion. Let it sit a while. Then come back and review and see what insights you have about your questions.

Journey

What is the answer to my question?

Silence

Silence is essential.
We need silence
just as much as we need air,
just as much as plants need light.
If our minds are crowded
with words and thoughts,
there is no space for us.

—Thich Nhat Hanh

Is silence a natural respite for you or something you do your best to avoid? In silence, do you feel lonely or complete? We each experience silence differently. The absence of auditory distractions allows us to listen more carefully to our inner voice and to take a break from increasingly present "noise pollution," which can wear on our senses even if we don't realize it. Find some time to be in silence today and note how you react.

Journey

Experience silence.

Service in the Community

Life's most persistent
and urgent question is,
"What are you doing for others?"
—Dr. Martin Luther King Jr.

We play different roles in the varying circles we move through: home, work, social, community. We're called to help in different ways, such as taking an active role, being a steadying presence, or even stepping back and letting someone else have the opportunity to step up. Today, we ask for guidance about your role in the community.

Journey

How can I best serve in my community today?

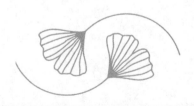

Rest Your Body

*Sleep gives us a chance
to refocus on the essence
of who we are.*

—Arianna Huffington

What would soothe and refresh your physical body today? Let the wisdom of your body, and your helping spirits, guide you in choosing how to spend your rest time today. Listen to your body about what kind of rest you need today. Don't overthink it. Maybe what's needed is a nap. It's also possible that the most restful thing for your body would be a gentle walk or a massage.

Journey

For your journey today, ask for guidance about what your body needs for rest and then do it.

Overlooked Abundance

Not what we have
but what we enjoy,
constitutes our abundance.

—Epicurus

When we hear the word "abundance," we often think of material abundance, but there are many intangible forms of abundance, too. Perhaps you have an abundance of perseverance that helps get you through challenging times. An abundance of that sort might actually be more of a blessing. Today let's ask if there is something we have in abundance that we tend to overlook.

Journey

Where is there abundance in my life that I have overlooked?

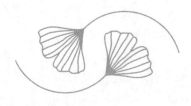

Truth

They say
the two most important days
in a person's life
were the day you were born
and the day you discover
why you were born.

—Viola Davis

What would your life be like if you knew what was true and what was false? Today, we are asking for help sensing and uncovering truth, with the intention that this heightened sense be used only for the highest good. This is not about other people's business or even knowing everything about our own lives, but asking for help refining our "truth" sense.

Journey

Please help me discern truth in my life today.

Appreciation

There is more hunger
for love and appreciation
in this world
than for bread.

—MOTHER TERESA

What do you appreciate about yourself? Ask for guidance if you are genuinely struggling with this. Try to go beyond the superficial. Find one thing or many things, and then spend time truly appreciating yourself today. The power of spiritual practices is not in the short bursts when we are journeying or meditating but in the changes they inspire in the remaining hours of the day. Try to carry the energy of self-appreciation that you are seeding from within your journey throughout your day. For example, if you are guided to appreciate your perseverance and your kindness, you may be shown ways in your life that those qualities have been present and meaningful. And then for the rest of the day perhaps you could find ways to express those qualities, and to appreciate yourself for them, with more awareness.

Journey

Appreciate yourself.

Stop Saying That

*What we speak
becomes the house
we live in.*

—Hafez

The language that we use plays a significant part in creating our perception of the world. Are there any words or phrases that you should stop using (or use more selectively) to create the world you wish to experience?

Journey

Are there any words or phrases I should stop using?

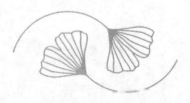

Singing

Singing
has always seemed to me
the most perfect means of expression.

—Georgia O'Keeffe

Singing and storytelling are both powerful traditions in all cultures. Today, we combine them as we sing the stories of our journeys. Journey wherever, and about whatever topic you wish. Try narrating your journey with song as you journey. This may take a moment to get used to if you usually journey silently. Shamans from indigenous cultures would often narrate their experience from within their trance states while they moved, conveying with words and actions what the spirits were showing and telling them, often with the help of an assistant.

Journey

Sing your journey today.

Earth/Below

We call in and honor the spirits of the Earth:
Of all the animals and plants
The land and elements
The web that sustains and nourishes us.

—Invocation

Acknowledging the directions is part of indigenous cultures from around the world. Before starting ceremonies, and as a daily practice, we can honor the spirit of the directions and welcome them to be present. This can be done silently or with rattling or drumming by facing the direction and giving thanks.*

I was given the invocation above when I asked my helping spirits for guidance about creating my own ceremony for honoring the directions. What is your relationship with the Earth? Is there an energy or feeling associated with that direction for you? One way to honor the Earth is with a wake-up prayer of gratitude.

Journey

Journey to the spirits of the Earth to ask how you can honor and get to know them better.

---

* More information about honoring the directions is in the Appendix in "Invocation: Welcoming the Spirits and Directions."

Time Off

I wish Americans
thought more like Europeans
when it comes to money and work.
They take time off,
they do what they love.
We think work
is the most valued commodity.
Really the most valued commodity
is time.

—BRYAN CRANSTON

Have you ever had a surprise day off with no agenda? No one asking anything from you, no responsibilities. For some people this sounds great. For others, the lack of structure is nerve-wracking. Which are you? I can't give you a day off from your job, but think about the concept, and try to take some time off today in whatever way you can, even if that is a day off from your spiritual practice. Sabbaticals can be power times to reframe and recharge.

Journey

Either take time off from journeying and have a micro-sabbatical today or journey on how to create meaningful time off for yourself.

Dream Theme

Anyone who dreams
partakes in shamanism.

—STANLEY KRIPPNER

My dreams are populated with lifelong themes, patterns that come in phases, and occasional star appearances. They have horrified me with epic perils, delighted me with playful visitations, introduced me to power animals, and warned me of danger in waking life. What are your dreams like?

Dream states, and the hypnagogic times just before and after sleep, are fertile ground for personal insights, creative inspiration, and scientific breakthroughs. When we pay attention to the information in our dreams, much can be learned. This is especially true for dream themes or patterns. What are your most frequent recurring dream themes? Think of a dream theme to explore with your helping spirits.

Journey

What is my dream theme showing me?

Gathering Nuts

*The thrill of not knowing
what's going to happen,
trained me to be prepared
for anything.*

—ARIANA GRANDE

Squirrels obsessively gather and bury nuts, preparing for winter. Nature provides them with the instinct to prepare to stay well. It's often harder for us to prepare for what comes next. We generally have the benefit of not worrying about our very immediate survival and the challenge of focusing on more complex and less predictable issues. It's still good to check in.

Journey

Is there anything I need to gather, literally or metaphorically, to prepare for what comes next?

Ideal Relationships

Nowhere else
is there such intimate
and frightening access
to the mysterium.
Friendship is the sweet grace
that liberates us to approach,
recognize and inhabit
this adventure.

—JOHN O'DONOHUE

Think of a relationship, whichever is the first to come to mind. What do you want to see in that relationship (healing, peace, cooperation)? Keep it positive. In today's journey, experience that relationship with all your senses as if it is already exactly like your ideal vision.

Journey

Vision a relationship in its ideal state.

Favorite Place

It is not down in any map;
true places never are.

—HERMAN MELVILLE

Do you have a place that you love? Maybe a real place in nature, or a place you go in your mind when you meditate or journey. Just as with our relationships with other beings, we can also develop a relationship with place. Returning to that place can be like returning to visit an old friend who knows and loves you. We can miss places like we miss people and animals. Today, let's journey to one of those places and spend some quality time.

Journey

Journey to a place you love and spend time.

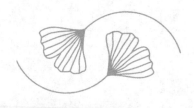

Ancestors

Every time a shaman dies,
it is as if a library burned down.

—MARK PLOTKIN

Today's journey is devoted to our biological ancestors. Pick one you knew growing up, or one you wish you knew better. Send them love and appreciation.

Journey

Journey to honor an ancestor today.

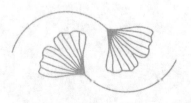

Anxiety Antidote

*Our anxiety does not come
from thinking about the future,
but from wanting to control it.*

—KHALIL GIBRAN

When the external world is intense, we often experience that intensity internally as angst or uneasiness. Having techniques that act as antidotes to these sensations is helpful. Ask for methods to use on your own, or simply for energetic help. What can I do to calm anxiety in my body and mind today? Let's envision that calm already here.

Journey

Spirits, thank you for helping to bring calm to my body and mind today.

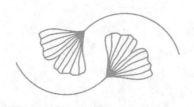

Open Heart

Conceptual knowledge
is so valued in our world.
Yet in many cultures
wisdom is equated
not with knowledge
but with an open heart.

—ROSHI JOAN HALIFAX

Shamans are sometimes described as people who "see with their hearts." What might change for you if you saw with your heart? Perceiving the world from different perspectives can help keep us flexible and invite positive change into our lives.

Journey

Journey to ask for help seeing with your heart.

What Needs Hearing?

> *If we surrendered*
> *to earth's intelligence,*
> *we could rise up rooted,*
> *like trees.*
>
> —RAINER MARIA RILKE

What we ask is naturally bound to our awareness. When we ask to be told what we need to hear, we give the helping spirits permission to provide guidance beyond the scope of what we may conceive of asking them. This can be surprising and powerful.

Journey

Please tell me what I need to hear.

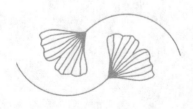

Water Creatures

Legend tells us
that the salmon were people
shaped like us
that lived in a beautiful city
below the ocean floor.
The Spirit of the Salmon People
chose to come back every spring and fall
to feed the two legged of this world.

—AGNES BAKER PILGRIM

One way to expand our perception of the world is to see from perspectives outside our usual vantage point. This can help us process information in new ways and learn something about ourselves. It can also help us live more harmoniously with other beings. In this journey, let's delve outside our element and slip into the world of water.

Journey

Journey to experience the world from a water creature's point of view.

Belief into Action

If you are neutral
in situations of injustice,
you have chosen
the side of the oppressor.
If an elephant has its foot
on the tail of a mouse
and you say that you are neutral,
the mouse will not appreciate
your neutrality.

—DESMOND TUTU

Individuals making small choices for positive change can make large collective impacts. Small actions ripple out to create larger waves.

Journey

How can I put my beliefs into action today?

Next Steps

*Meditate
on the things you are doing
as being already done—
complete and perfect.*

—ERNEST HOLMES

Let's ask this next question with no prelude and see what comes.

Journey

What are the next steps in my personal evolution?

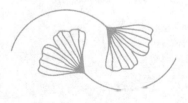

Play Break

A little nonsense
now and then
is relished
by the wisest men.

—WILLY WONKA

The opportunity for play is everywhere. Even animals that spend virtually all their waking hours looking for food to survive seem to manage time to enjoy themselves once in a while. Somehow, someway, infuse your day with a little play today. Whether through a playful conversation or text exchange, watching a funny show by yourself, or playing a game with a pet or child, ease whatever burdens you feel with some lightness today.

Journey

Either journey and have some playtime in non-ordinary reality, or use your practice time today to do something light and playful in ordinary reality.

Ceremony to Honor Someone

Spirit
guides me in all my work.
Basically, my teaching
is to be human,
honor people,
and be free in the heart.

—GRANDMOTHER FLOREMAYO

Think about someone who has significantly impacted your life. Whether or not you've overtly recognized that person or told them how you feel before, today is about acknowledging them.

Journey

Create a ceremony in ordinary or non-ordinary reality to honor someone who has significantly impacted your life.

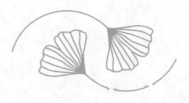

Visioning

*Every great dream
begins with
a dreamer.*

—HARRIET TUBMAN

Focus on a dream or vision that you wish to see unfold in your life. In your journey or meditation today, experience that dream as if it has already happened. Use all your senses. Experience it in the present moment. Feel it, see it, smell it, taste it. Imagine talking about it with your friends. What are you doing, what are you seeing, what are you wearing, what can you smell and touch? Feel the satisfaction of having it in your life now.

Journey

Journey to experience your vision.

Vision into Action

*If you are working
on something exciting
that you really care about,
you don't have to be pushed.
The vision pulls you.*

—STEVE JOBS

In the full sensory experience of visioning in yesterday's journey, you tapped into the power of working in the invisible realm. Let's support that work with concrete action to bring it more tangibly into the visible realm.

Journey

Please show me some practical, manageable steps I can take now to bring my vision into the world.

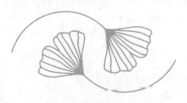

Life Goals

*Hope is not what we find
in evidence,
it's what we become
in action.*

—Frances Moore Lappé

Do you spend time thinking about big goals you hope to accomplish? Let's ask if there are larger lessons or goals for this lifetime that have been overlooked, or that need particular attention now. These may fall under various headings, like practical, interpersonal, or spiritual. And even though these are "big" as they span a lifetime, they can also be "small" in scale, such as stopping to appreciate beauty in the everyday, or making time for your friends. This doesn't have to be the type of bucket list that includes winning the Nobel Prize or climbing Mt. Everest!

Journey

Journey to ask your helping spirits for guidance about your lifetime lessons and goals.

Perceiving Divine Presence

*The Goddess is not just a light, happy maiden
or a nurturing mother.
She is death as well as birth,
dark as well as light,
rage as well as compassion—
and if we shy away
from her fiercer embrace,
we undercut both her own power
and our own growth.*

—STARHAWK

The divine surrounds us and is within us all the time; but it can be easy to forget that, and to feel disconnected and alone. There are many ways to feel more connected when we are intentional, like journeying, prayer, or being in nature. But wouldn't it be nice to have a reminder of that divine presence as we went about our day? A code word or sign that pointed out the divine in ordinary reality would serve as a tap on the shoulder when we need to be reminded that we're not alone.

Journey

How can I perceive the presence of the divine in the everyday?

Dwelling in the Past

*It feels like
old knowledge:
to grieve properly,
we first need
to face reality.*

—Leah Penniman

Do you replay past events in your mind's eye? How often are they positive, and how often are they about regret or heartache? Which of these replays of the past is it time to let go of right now?

Journey

What is it time to let go of from the past?

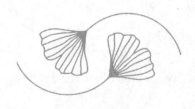

Physical Health

Treatment originates
outside you;
healing comes
from within.

—Dr. Andrew Weil

We count on our bodies perhaps more than anything else. Sometimes underappreciated, sometimes overemphasized, they are foundational to our experience in the world. Having a healthy body makes it easier to have a healthy mind and spirit. There are many concrete steps we take in ordinary reality to maintain our health. Let's also plant an intention of robust physical health in non-ordinary reality today. As you speak the words of this intention for health, you will be aligning the visible and the invisible, each supporting the other.

Journey

In your journey today, use the mantra "I am physically healthy and strong."

Shifting Gears

As an adventurer
the shaman was trained to be flexible,
to be comfortable with change
and to direct it in a positive way,
to be free to explore
new ways and means of doing things . . .
—Serge Kahili King

If you've ever driven a car with a manual transmission, you know that changing gears takes a little practice. The interplay between the gas and the clutch when shifting is important. Those micro-moments of change in driving are not dissimilar to "shifting gears" in our lives. We need time to transition gracefully, neither gunning it recklessly into the next thing, nor stalling out in indecision or inertia. Sometimes we don't allow ourselves adequate time to process transitions. Is there any area where you need more time to shift gears before moving into the next phase?

Journey

Please guide me in shifting gears as smoothly as possible.

Mental Energy

The highest possible stage
in moral culture
is when we recognize
that we ought to control
our thoughts.

—CHARLES DARWIN

Our power goes where our thoughts are focused. Our thoughts affect the tone of our inner world, how we relate to others, and what we can accomplish. Harnessing our mental energy is extremely powerful and can be a challenge.

Journey

Where should I focus my mental energy today?

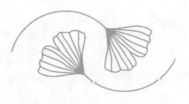

Sense of Safety

*There are times
to shiver and run
and there are times
to not.*

—CLARISSA PINKOLA ESTÉS

Our sense of safety operates on many levels, including phys-ical, emotional, and financial. We have our individual pri-orities, history, and triggers around issues of safety, but we all want to experience a feeling of safety in our lives.

Journey

What do I need to feel safe?

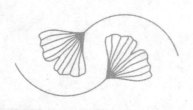

Conscious Cooking

*Our lives are not
in the lap of the gods,
but in the lap
of our cooks.*

—LIN YUTANG

I have a friend who cooks with love. She prays as she cooks. She infuses each dish with divine energy, and it's tangible; when you eat her food you feel loved, you feel cared for. The ingredients and recipes are tasty, but the intention that she holds while preparing the food imbues it with energy that takes the nourishment to a whole new level. Let's cook with love. Whether you are cooking for a crowd or having a solitary meal, try using your prep time as a meditation. Here are some ideas: as you stir, say a loving mantra; as you chop, envision healing energy radiating from your hands; or, as you bake, infuse each ingredient with caring thoughts. Let's ask the helping spirits for some more ideas.

Journey

How can I prepare food with love?

With Thanks

We can only be said to be alive
in those moments
when our hearts are conscious
of our treasures.

—THORNTON WILDER

Let's remember to give and receive thanks. For those who contributed in ways we know of, for those who work anonymously on our behalf, for the work we do. For those long past, for those with us today, for the generations yet to come; may we be grateful for our place in our lineage, and do our best to be worthy of gratitude. In today's journey express gratitude and then be open to receive it.

Journey

Through a quiet period of prayer or meditation, or through a formal journey to ask your helping spirits to assist you, spend time today specifically offering your gratitude to others, and then receive the gratitude that the spirits show you is there for you to receive.

Grace

*You can have
the other words—
chance, luck, coincidence, serendipity.
I'll take grace.
I don't know what it is exactly,
but I'll take it.*

—MARY OLIVER

One definition of grace is "the love and mercy given to us by God because God desires us to have it, not because of anything we have done to earn it." This unmerited divine assistance can appear in our lives in subtle and dramatic ways. It can seem sporadic, yet it is there all the time waiting for us to recognize its beautiful presence.

Journey

Journey to a helping spirit and ask, "How is grace working in my life right now?"

Time Management

*The key
is not to prioritize
what's on your schedule,
but to schedule
your priorities.*

—STEPHEN COVEY

What is your relationship to time? Do you find yourself with not enough or too much? What we're doing and when we do it can make a huge difference in how we perceive time. For example, I'm typically active and ready to go in the mornings. Afternoons are a slow time for me. If I need to write or do creative work that takes a lot of focused mental energy, mornings are generally better. Thinking ahead to manage my use of time helps the day (and time) flow better. What works best for you?

Journey

How can I best relate to time throughout the day?

Giving and Receiving

I realize that
everything is happening to everyone
collectively,
and I feel appreciation
and compassion
for us all.

—SYLVIA BOORSTEIN

Every healthy system has a balance between energy in and energy out. In many different areas of our lives, a balance of giving and receiving helps us to stay healthy, too; work, family, friendships, communication, how you relax and exert yourself. Do your systems feel in balance? If not, what can you do to recalibrate?

Journey

Please show me how to create a good balance of giving and receiving today.

Processing New Information

*Learning
is the only thing
the mind never exhausts,
never fears,
and never regrets.*

—LEONARDO DA VINCI

Particularly as we get older, it can be harder to take in and process new information, change our opinions, and expand in ways that might be uncomfortable. Sometimes this is exactly what we need to grow and evolve. Perhaps there are ways to take in new information that will help make the process as stress-free as possible for you.

Journey

Journey to ask for ways to take in new information gracefully.

Gender and Gender Identity

As far as I'm concerned,
being any gender
is a drag.

—Patti Smith

Gender is a very complex topic. A mix of biological, famil-ial, cultural, institutional, and very personal factors go into our experience of ourselves and the idea of gender and gen-der identity. Because it is so fundamental to who we are as individuals, it can be hard to imagine seeing the world from a different viewpoint. Let's explore that today.

Journey

Journey for insight into what it would be like to be a gender other than your own.

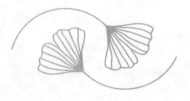

Step Up, Step Back

Loud men
should study meditation;
quiet women
should attend shouting classes.

—Sparrow

Have you ever been in a group (a meeting, a class, a family gathering, a dinner party) where a few people dominated the conversation and others hardly said anything? What are your reactions to that dynamic? Are you ever one of the people speaking up frequently or rarely? When we are taking up too much space (literally, verbally, energetically) maybe it's time to take a step back and make room for others to step up. Or vice versa, despite the discomfort of stepping up, maybe it's time.

In order to be in good relation with others in different groups, and to understand our natural tendencies, it's helpful to get perspective and clarity about this. Our helping spirits, with their honestly and kindness, are a good resource for feedback.

Journey

Are there areas where I need to step up and/or step back?

Different Ways to Rest

The more relaxed you are,
the better you are at everything:
the better you are with your loved ones,
the better you are with your enemies,
the better you are at your job,
the better you are with yourself.

—BILL MURRAY

Sometimes we need total rest, and sometimes it's specific aspects of who we are that need downtime. For example, we may need physical rest when recovering from an accident or illness, yet crave intellectual stimulation; or, we may be mentally taxed from long hours at work and need a good long hike for our bodies to feel refreshed. On your journey today, be open to these different definitions of rest while you get information about the kind of rest your whole being needs most right now.

Journey

For your journey today, ask for guidance about what your whole being needs for rest and then do it.

Alleviating Suffering

Mankind
at its most desperate
is often at its best.

—Bob Geldof

For sensitive people in particular, to tap into the incredible suffering in the world today can feel overwhelming. This can be paralyzing, especially if we are also dealing with personal pain. Let's ask for help identifying manageable ways, in the visible or invisible realms, where we can help alleviate suffering today.

Journey

How can I help alleviate suffering today?

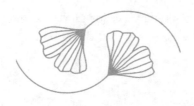

Ancient Water

Water symbolizes
the whole of potentiality—
the source of all possible existence.

—MIRCEA ELIADE

Water has been here for millions of years. Life teemed in the oceans long before we were formed. Water issues are common today; much of our water is polluted, some areas are flooded, and others are in drought. Ask your helping spirits to take you to the ancient waters. What can you learn from the ancient water itself?

Journey

Journey to ancient water.

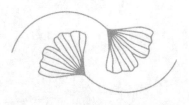

Courage

I have learned
over the years
that when one's mind is made up,
this diminishes fear;
knowing what must be done
does away with fear.

—ROSA PARKS

Have you ever faced a situation that called for bravery but felt you were running a little short?

Journey

Ask your helping spirits to give you a ritual or ceremony to perform when you need courage.

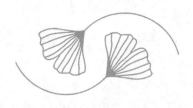

Back in Time
to Love Yourself as an Adult

I do not trust people
who don't love themselves
and yet tell me,
"I love you."
There is an African saying which is:
Be careful when a naked person
offers you a shirt.

—MAYA ANGELOU

Wherever you are in your adult life, pick an earlier time when you could have used some guidance, a shoulder, reassurance, or just a loving word.

Journey

Journey to a time earlier in your adult life and offer yourself support.

Anticipation

"Well," said Pooh, "what I like best,"
and then he had to stop and think.
Because although Eating Honey
was a very good thing to do,
there was a moment
just before you began to eat it
which was better than when you were,
but he didn't know
what it was called.

—A. A. Milne

Are you able to delay gratification or do you eat dessert first? Particularly if the latter is true, how can you make the most of the energy of anticipation? How can you enjoy the anticipation of whatever life has to offer you in the future, while savoring the present moment?

Journey

Journey for guidance about sinking into anticipation.

Miracles

Miracles are a retelling
in small letters
of the very same story
which is written
across the whole world
in letters too large
for some of us to see.

—C. S. LEWIS

Do you believe in miracles? Do you seek the miraculous in your life? Some people experience amazing things and discount them, others find awe in everyday "miracles." Let's ask for guidance about our relationship with miracles.

Journey

How can I encourage miracles in my life and recognize them when they arrive?

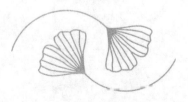

Abundance

Both abundance and lack
exist simultaneously in our lives,
as parallel realities.
It is always our conscious choice
which secret garden
we will tend.

—SARAH BAN BREATHNACH

It's easy to slip into states of consciousness that focus on what is lacking. Today, let's remind ourselves of what we have in abundance.

Journey

Give thanks for what is abundant in your life.

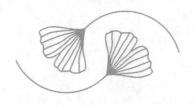

Planning for the Down Slope

*Going through
an intensive experience
only to return inward
can evoke emptiness,
anxiety, loss and loneliness,
but these feelings can inspire curiosity
about the next stage.*

—ORNA GURALINK

After big events it's not uncommon to feel a letdown. We build up to the event, time and energy are spent, and we get worn out. Emotions have often run a little high. When it's done, you may feel a rosy afterglow or huge relief that something stressful is behind you. We're more likely to crash and get sick or sad on these downslope times when things are sliding back to baseline after something big. Whether you have a big event coming up, have just finished with one, or can think of a time in the future that you might plan for, let's think of the best ways to handle this time on the down slope.

Journey

Journey and ask, "How can I best prepare to take care of myself on the down slope after big events?"

Center/Within

We call in and honor
the spirits of the Center:
Of the void
Of all possibilities
Of the mystery,
and the divine within each of us

—INVOCATION

Acknowledging the directions is part of indigenous cultures from around the world. Before starting ceremonies, and as a daily practice, we can honor the spirit of the directions and welcome them to be present. This can be done silently or with rattling or drumming by facing the direction and giving thanks.*

I was given the invocation above when I asked my helping spirits for guidance about creating my own ceremony for honoring the directions. What is your relationship with the center or within? Is there an energy or feeling associated with that direction for you? One way to honor the spirit within is by caring for yourself gently today.

Journey

Journey to the spirits of the Center to ask how you can honor and get to know them better.

---

* More information about honoring the directions is in the Appendix in "Invocation: Welcoming the Spirits and Directions."

Open Guidance

The thing that makes you exceptional,
if you are at all,
is inevitably that which
must also make you lonely.

—Lorraine Hansberry

Asking specific questions creates a clear intention and is powerful. Today, we balance structure and flow by leaving our question open.

Journey

What do I need to know today?

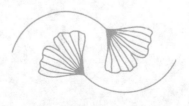

Remembering

Listen to the silence
inside the illusion of the world,
and you will remember
the lesson you forgot.

—Jack Kerouac

Occasionally I forget things. Sometimes they are small things; other times, big things, like lessons I thought I'd learned a long time ago. Does this ever happen to you? Sometimes a gentle reminder is all we need.

Journey

Please remind me if there is something I've forgotten that is important to know now.

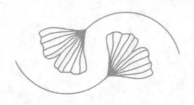

Imagining Your Dream to Life

*Imagination is
when you pretend something
until it is true.*

—PHILIP KENNER, *age 6*

What is your most dearly held dream? Maybe it's the dream you don't share because it is too precious to speak out loud. Or maybe it's the one you talk about *constantly* because you are obsessed! In ordinary and non-ordinary reality, let's bring your dream to life. In your journey, use all the power of your imagination to feel your dream as if it is already here.

Journey

Use all your internal senses to experience your dream: see it, feel it, even smell it. Imagine talking about it with your family.

Then, in your ordinary reality life, take one small practical step to bring you closer to the realization of your dream.

Expanding Your Practice

Invocation: Welcoming the Spirits and Directions

"RATTLING IN THE SPIRITS" is a deliberate practice of honoring the spiritual beings we share space with, and asking them to be present for our work. It can be done prior to a single journey or before a larger ceremony. "Rattling in" is actually more of a recognition than a summoning. All around us, to the East and West, to the North and South, to the Sky above, and to the Earth below, we are connected to others in body and spirit. From the Center—our center and the mysterious center of all that is—we find our place. As we turn and rattle in each of the directions, we are expressing our gratitude and honing our awareness of our place within the multidimensional sphere of existence. Different traditions ascribe different qualities to the directions. The invocation given to me is below. As you create your own relationship, you may wish to design your own invocation for welcoming the spirits. You may do this silently or out loud. With your invocation, the power is in your intention and focus rather than how you string together the words. It is your choice whether you do this before journeying or mostly with longer ceremonies. Perhaps you will consult your helping spirits and be shown a different way to begin your ceremonies, or follow this structure but create new language.

We welcome and honor the spirits of the East:
> *Of beginnings and hope*
> *Of spring and new life*

We welcome and honor the spirits of the South:
> *Of fertility and creativity*
> *Of warmth and abundance*

We welcome and honor the spirits of the West:
> *Of adventure and strength*
> *Of expansiveness and transformation*

We welcome and honor the spirits of the North:
> *Of power and fortitude*
> *Of deep rest and stillness*

We welcome and honor the spirits of the Heavens:
> *The celestial beings and divine guidance*
> *The canopy that protects and embraces us*

We welcome and honor the spirits of the Earth:
> *Of all the animals and plants*
> *The land and elements*
> *The web that sustains and nourishes us*

We welcome and honor the spirits of the Center:
> *Of the void*
> *Of all possibilities*
> *Of the mystery*
> *And of the divine within each of us.*

Ceremonies and Rituals

Ceremonies are universal; all cultures have them. Some we do alone and some involve hundreds, even thousands, of people. Ceremonies can be elaborate or very simple. Some have centuries of tradition, with very specific rules and steps (think Japanese tea ceremonies, royal weddings, bar mitzvahs, and the Diné Blessingway.) Others are very simple (think saying grace before eating, crossing oneself with holy water as you walk into a Catholic church, lighting a candle while saying a prayer, and smudging yourself or a room).

Simple ceremonies might more accurately be thought of as rituals. Rituals are often incorporated into our daily life to infuse it with meaning and intention. They help remind us to match our actions with our beliefs and to shift our state of mind to match what we are doing or trying to accomplish. Ceremonies are done for particular outcomes or events, rather than something that you do every day.

Ceremonies mark changes of seasons, phases of life, accomplishments, and dreams. They are used in times of great happiness, sadness, union, dissolution, beginnings, and endings. They are performed to honor and bless. They can be particularly powerful for healing and evolution when crafted in partnership with helping spirits and performed with intention and focus. We are weaving the visible and the invisible worlds into new realities when we work with ceremony and ritual.

What follows is a detailed approach to designing your own ceremony. All good ceremonies have a clear beginning, middle, and end. And they have a strong intention, like a mission statement, with all elements supporting that intention. Keep those two things in mind, and whether your ceremony is short, simple, and solo, or long, complex, and including many people, you'll have a good foundation.

Design your own ceremonies

One of my helping spirits gave me an analogy to help me think about the different styles of ceremonies. Preparing for ceremonies can be like planning a lovely gathering with a delicious meal; there are many ways to do it well.

Some are spontaneous and personal, just for you. You improvise, and the experience is ephemeral. Maybe you make something delicious for the first time that you create with a new ingredient you found, or a unique combination of odds and ends in the fridge that came together in some alchemical harmony. Maybe you eat in your comfiest chair, or sitting outside on the grass, or even standing at the counter in your kitchen. These can be powerful and beautiful events.

However, a lovely gathering and meal, whether for one, two, ten, or more, usually takes some planning, and so does an effective ceremony. Just as you decide what mood you are trying to create with your meal, choosing the flavors and dishes that are most appropriate, you determine what is the intention, or purpose, of the ceremony, and chose those elements with equal care. In a shamanic ceremony, you will want to consult with your helping spirits along the way for guidance and advice. With a family celebration, there is often collaboration as well. You think about what foods you'd like to serve that match the mood and event you are celebrating. You decide who is invited, where it will

410

be held, and when it will begin. These decisions are relevant to designing good ceremonies as well, and should align with the intention of your ceremony. Everything should follow from, and align with, your ceremony's intention. It's like the mission statement for the event. If you are honoring a friend's successful transition out of a damaging relationship and into a healthier one, you probably won't invite people who trigger his trauma. If your ceremony is to welcome in spring, you probably won't hold it in December. If you are holding a healing ceremony for a sick child, you hopefully won't choose a nightclub as your venue.

Once you decide the intention, and the who, what, where, and when, you prepare. With a special meal, a few days before the gathering you would have shopped for the ingredients and anything else you need to serve or set the mood like candles, wine, or games. For your ceremony, you will gather your supplies, make your ceremonial objects, and make sure you have everything you need at hand prior to starting. These are the visible things that serve the invisible intention.

For your meal, well before your guests arrive (or before you want to start if it is a solo ceremony), you've tended to the space, cleaning and clearing clutter. Closer to the time of the event, you've taken a shower or bath and put on something that you particularly like to wear. You'll do the same for your ceremonial space, cleansing it and yourself, both physically and energetically, perhaps smudging with sage, incense, or oils.

As your guests are about to arrive, you light candles and put on music. You put a clean tablecloth on the table. As the table is often the center of focus for a special meal, so an altar is the focus of a ceremony. This can be as simple as a lit candle on a small table. Think about where the focal point of your ceremony will be. How can you create an altar that is appropriate and powerful for your ceremonial work?

Once everyone has arrived you have a period before the meal (ceremony) with some chatting to shift the energy and have everyone get comfortable before they move into the dining room or outside to the patio or wherever you will be serving the special meal. This holds true for most ceremonies, too. If others are to join you for your ceremony, you'll want to have a little transition time. It's your ceremony, so you set the tone. If you want people to be serious and silent, let that be known. If laughter and joking are okay, let that be known as well. As the master of ceremonies, you will want to convey, through your words, actions, and preparedness, the intention of the ceremony. Others can then follow you with ease and hold the power of the ceremony strong.

Once you are ready to serve, you signal that the meal is about to begin. Perhaps you ring a little bell or chime, or just call people in to start. Possibly there is a time to say grace or express appreciation and thankfulness for the food that is spread on the table. Maybe you toast good wishes to everyone's health, to the host, or to whoever is being honored by the occasional, or just to life! *L'chaim!* In the language of ceremony, this is the invocation. At the beginning, as the power of attention is high, you will want to state the intention of your ceremony. What are you invoking, why are you here, who are you asking to help. You give thanks. The ceremony has officially begun.

We all know the tools of the ceremony of eating! In different cultures we use different tools, and it works out.

412

There are plates and platters, for ourselves and to share. Sometimes we are served individually. Sometimes from a communal plate. We use forks, knives, spoons, chopsticks, and our hands. We eat and drink and talk. Sometimes there are many courses. Sometimes just one. Sometimes the food itself is symbolic, like matzoh at the Passover seder. (The seder is a perfect example of a ceremonial meal, where each moment, each act, each object, each food, each spoken word, individually and collectively, has a deep meaning that goes back many generations.)

And then there is the closing, maybe the sweetness of dessert, cheese, or an aperitif. We are full, physically with delicious sustaining food, emotionally with the interactions and conversations we've had, and spiritually with what it means symbolically to come together and celebrate.

All of these aspects of sharing a meal are relevant when you think about designing a ceremony for a group, too. How can people participate and build the power of the collective energy? What are the stages and how do they complement each other? How simple do you want the ceremony to be? Simple is often best. Might you want to add something a little sweet at the end to close?

———∞∞∞———

Here is a condensed version of a ceremony prep list:

- Preparation (internal and external preparation, materials, altar, intention ready, invocation ready, cleaning energy and clearing mind)

- Beginning (intention set, invocation, welcoming/thanking helping spirits, boundaries and safe space established)
- Middle (the actual steps of your ceremony)
- Ending (thank-you, grounding, closing, celebration)

Ceremony preparation journeys

Creating your own ceremonies is a collaborative process between you and your spiritual support. As you've likely discovered, what our logical, ego-based selves want is not always the same as what our intuitive or spiritual guidance suggests. Ideally, we honor both. Here are a few journey ideas that can help you design ceremonies that are both energetically powerful and practical to create and perform:

What would be an auspicious/helpful ceremony to do now?

Please help me design a ceremony for _____ .

How can I best support this intention?

What materials will I need?

Where and when would be best to perform the ceremony?

What internal preparation will I need to do to be ready to perform this ceremony?

Deeper Experiences

The daily journeys seed consistent practice. There are also times when we want to stay with a particular theme and go deeper. We do multiple journeys, returning to get a fuller picture, and seeing the issue from multiple angles. What follows are a few suggestions for these deeper experiences.

Practice seeing in the dark: Shamanic sensing

To engage the power of shamanism in your daily life, you can practice "seeing in the dark." That practice begins with small, simple steps. Ultimately, to create meaningful change, it also needs to include holding focus, expanding perception, and adjusting the way you look at the world. Here's an example that illustrates how this works with physical vision. We're used to looking straight ahead to try to see more clearly, but when it's dark you can actually see more with your peripheral vision than when you look straight on. If you're looking at a beautiful starry sky, you can see more stars if you focus softly around the edges. This example involves a physical sense organ, but the ability to perceive using subtle senses works similarly; sometimes softer, less direct way of engaging allow you to perceive more.

In your journeys, rather than focusing on *trying* to have a vision or perceive energetically, let your sensing soften, let your field of focus widen. What do you sense when you are not "seeing" in the usual ways? Being able to shift your vision to suit the purpose of what you are trying to see is a shamanic skill. Some things are actually *easier* to see in the dark. We all have the capacity to perceive with our whole being. It may take some practice and time, but you *can* shift your vision to perceive more like a shaman.

Pay particular attention to ways you can see with the more subtle senses. We are using the word "see" as a catchall for sensing. When a shaman sees in the dark she isn't necessarily receiving visual information; she may be having a physical sensation, hearing words, or experiencing a knowing. These are perfectly valid ways of "seeing with shaman's eyes." This can also be described as intuition, like the classic "gut feeling."

Journey

Please show me how to "see in the dark."

<hr>

Most profound changes come when we are bringing new awareness into our everyday activities, not just the moments of spiritual practice. What would it be like if you shut your eyes and explored what you "saw" while in different environments, or if you shifted to see things through the lens of your heart rather than your head?

<hr>

Additional journeys from *Daily Journeys* on this theme of shamanic perception:

- 41 What Needs Seeing?
- 67 Clear Sight
- 69 Dream Guidance
- 85 Animal Spirit Sight
- 140 Bird's-Eye View
- 264 Insect Eyes

Intention

I am able to see in the dark.

Be nature: reciprocity and health

Whether it's planting a garden, walking in the woods, or being immersed in wilderness, nature is nourishing at a deep level. As with many things we've known instinctually and experientially for ages, science is confirming the health benefits of being in nature. The Japanese practice of *shinrin-yoku* or forest bathing—what a delightful image!—is simply walking in the forest or a natural environment. Studies show it lowers blood pressure, pulse rates, and cortisol levels. Additional research demonstrates that immersion in nature allows us to regain mental clarity and heal better after surgery. However, in shamanism it is important that we're not only receiving from nature, but that we understand at a fundamental level we *are* nature, intrinsically connected to all that is around us, and that we act accordingly.

Mutual exchange is important in relationships of all kinds. The idea of reciprocity with nature, of treating the Earth and the creatures we share her with as family, is a basic premise of shamanism. In Andean cultures, like the Quecha and Aymara, the word *ayni* refers to this idea of sacred reciprocity, taking care of one another for mutual benefit and out of love and respect. Eurasian shamanic societies, and indeed many other traditional cultures and religions, have clearly articulated ideas about how to live in balance with the natural world.

To form meaningful relationships of any kind, we first need an introduction. Then we begin communicating and taking the relationship deeper. Let's start locally. Where do you live? Whether in the city, the country, or somewhere in between, the land that you live on is "spirited." That land has an energy and spirit of its own. The land we live on hosts us as we move about the business of our lives, supporting us physically and energetically. It has its own history and its own character. As part of creating a respectful and healthy relationship with the world around us, it's helpful to acknowledge how the land we live (work, play, love) on has served us, and to offer thanks in return.

Journey

Journey to a spirit of the land on which you live. Introduce yourself and offer thanks. Ask for guidance about how to create a healthy reciprocal relationship.

———— ⚭ ————

You may find after this journey that the feeling of moving around in the environment in which you live shifts. Maybe you're inspired to greet the trees in the morning with a big hug, or give a subtle nod or a silent, *How's it going?* to an ancient being you've met. Perhaps you find that your place is a lot more populated than you thought! This can be exciting, or sometimes even disconcerting. There are so many more layers to the spiritual realms than most of us are used to engaging. A woman I worked with described the feeling she had when she first started journeying, "I'm reminded of when people thought the world was flat, then things opened up and expanded. There is so much to explore!"

As you move through your day, in non-journeying time, what would change if you thought of everything as being alive and inspirited: the water that you drink, the hills, the valleys, each plant in the understory of the forest, the storm front, the river, the little garden space behind your apartment building.

⊸∞∞⊷

Additional journeys from *Daily Journeys* that explore our relationships within the natural world:

- 14 Air
- 21 Heaven on Earth
- 71 Working with Fire
- 73 Environmental Supplements
- 75 Rain
- 321 Earth/Below

Intention

Nature is my family; we support each other.

Find calm in chaos: technology and spirit

Our relationship with time is changing. As social theorist Jeremy Rifkin puts it, we have become a "nanosecond culture." With currently accepted norms around the use of technology, it has become increasingly hard to pause, disconnect from the internet-based web and connect to the spirit-based web. We are expected to stay connected through our devices. While those devices, and the wealth of information and relationships that they can connect us to, have enriched our lives in many ways, they have contributed to a leaching in other ways. We are more readily connected to chaotic energies that are not our own. The web of life that is a basis for shamanism allows that everything is connected. We don't necessarily need the media to let us know if there is something out of balance in the world, but it makes it exponentially easier to feel that imbalance if it is delivered to us instantaneously with graphic imagery and sound bites.

The last few decades have been the early days of personal connectivity, the teen years so to speak. We—those of us who have access—have not been particularly discerning or disciplined about how we use these powerful media and tools for delivering such rich and complex content. Perhaps our shamanic practice can help inform us here.

Shamanism has staying power. It's the oldest known spiritual practice on the planet, and it is going strong today. Nothing lasts that long without evolving and adapting. Anthropologist Michael Harner said, "Shamanism isn't New Age, it's Stone Age." We can also argue that while shamanism has existed in *all* ages past, it will exist in whatever ages are coming in the future, because it evolves to fit the needs of current places and times.

From where I am writing, which is early 21st-century North America, we have some chaos to manage—internal and external chaos. It's overwhelming to try to tame wild, widespread external chaos, so let's start with each of us individually. It's the only place where change begins anyway. One of the basics of shamanic practice is a shift in consciousness. This can sound abstract. It is helpful to ease into it without pressure or expectation. It is easy to get frustrated with a spiritual practice when you want to still your thoughts, or have a profound vision, and your mind is running in circles. So stop, take a moment, put down the book, and take a few deep breaths, a pause from reading, or thinking that you have to do anything different at all. No really, do it right now please. . . . Thank you.

Calm can be elusive. Sometimes it's best to sneak up on it sideways. As I give you ideas for journeys or other thoughts for practicing, remember that you know what brings you peace and calm better than anyone else. What works for me may not for you, and vice versa. For example, I love animals, just about every kind. Holding a baby goat is my idea of heaven. They fall asleep on your lap, all floppy and warm. I could sit for hours, happy as can be. I was in a meeting the other day when someone shared that they are afraid of goats. So a lap goat would not elicit the calm state that we are going for. That person may find riding a Jet Ski to be calming and soothing in some way that I will never understand. Don't contort yourself to fit someone else's ideas about what being a spiritual, peaceful person is. Honor your own spirit, tend it, and give it space, even just a little every day, to be heard above the noise of our digitally and personally chaotic world. A few moments of peace and quiet spread throughout the day, when you are not doing anything, can be the opening for miraculous things to happen.

When chaos rules in your immediate environment, or in the greater world around you, it is easy to get caught up in the swirl of emotions and quickly changing circumstances. It becomes harder to keep your bearings, and stay true to your own core beliefs when so much is moving around you. The ability to stay calm in the midst of chaos, or regain calm if it is lost, is a particularly helpful tool. Let's ask for guidance about simple tools you can use if you find yourself swept up in the currents. In addition to guidance, the time in your journey can be to *experience* calm.

Journey

How can I stay calm in chaos? Experience calm within your journey.

⸺◦∞◦⸺

Even when you don't have time for a full journey or meditation, a few seconds to shift your attention can help to restore calm. If you work at a computer, perhaps set a reminder for once an hour and look out the window, or take a series of breaths, or get up and stretch. Get creative: take a minute or two of intentionally feeling your feet on the floor in the bathroom at work, or drink your tea really slowly so you feel each sip go down your throat, or stop and talk to a bird for a while. These things take no more than a minute and can start to bring a sense of calm.

⸺◦∞◦⸺

Additional journeys from *Daily Journeys* that explore the theme of staying calm:

- 64, 65, 66 Thriving in Chaos (three-journey series)
- 78 Managing Change and Volatility
- 82 Quick Calm
- 83 I Have Everything I Need
- 348 Time Management

Intention

I am calm and capable in any situation.

Navigate your energy ecosystem: spiritual boundaries

Indigenous cultures have a profound understanding of the interconnected web of life. As we evolve a deeper awareness of spiritual interconnection, we feel the experiences of our sisters and brothers (human, animal, and plant) more deeply, too. In order to be a healthy part of the web, we also need to find safety within ourselves. Each person is a unique ecosystem, with an innate energetic temperament. Relationships of two or more people create more complicated ecosystems, with more complex dynamics. Understanding how to navigate those energetic ecosystems is part of having healthy energetic boundaries.

Some people confuse our fundamental oneness with a need to be energetically wide open at all times; however, we need both states for our highest mental, emotional, and spiritual health. Differentiating self from others is "an important resilience factor," protecting us from experiencing others' trauma too intensely. Many people spend their lives wide open to others. In my practice as a shamanic and energy healing practitioner, I frequently see the aftermath of the absence of healthy boundaries—people who are exhausted, overwhelmed, stressed, maybe even depressed or burned out. Ironically, the empathic instinct of solidarity with our fellow beings becomes the very thing that prevents us from serving them—and ourselves—most effectively. When we establish a clear understanding of the difference between healthy compassion and draining empathy (very different experiences within the brain), we turn sensitivity into strength, for others and ourselves.

Journey

Ask a helping spirit to allow you to step into their field of energy to help you shore up your personal energetic boundary.

———— ∞ ————

Additional journeys from *Daily Journeys* that explore the theme of energy boundaries:

- 118 Boundaries of Forgiveness
- 122 Self-Compassion
- 162 Empathic Overload
- 163 Healthy Compassion
- 232 What Doesn't Belong?
- 291 Vulnerabilities

Intention

I am present and connected to others,
and safe and contained within my own energy body.

Moon Ceremonies and Journeys

Any time can be appropriate to do a moon ceremony; it's a matter of matching your intention to the moon's cycle.

Very simply put, the moon moves through phases, from new to waxing to full to waning and back to new again. Choosing when in the month to work is important, as you want to align your intention with the moon cycle and sync with the energy that is present already. You can think about the phases roughly like this: new (the beginning of a cycle), waxing (building energy, nurturing what has begun), full (seeing a phase come into completion), waning (take a pause for preparation to enter the next phase).

How might you work with these dynamics? For example, if you were creating a new venture, starting a new habit pattern or beginning a new relationship, working with the energy of the new moon would be ideal. The full moon is a powerful time for all ceremonies. Full moons are wonderful times to do blessing and healing ceremonies. Hospitals and police stations statistically see an uptick in activity during the full moon, as the energy gets intense. Often people don't know how to handle it productively. When you do, it can be potent.

These cycles may not exactly match your own relationship to the moon. Observe and see how you feel during the changing phases of the moon.

New Moon

NEW MOON, NEW ENERGY CEREMONY

Ask for (and then perform) a ceremony that helps you seed an intention for something new in your life. New moons are perfect times for putting power behind new projects or inspiring current ones. What do you want to unfold in your life right now? Ask to be shown the next steps and to have the power to take them. Go outside and be in the energy of the new moon.

Journey

Please show me a ceremony for empowering _____.

IDEAL WORK VISION

What do you want to unfold in your work right now? In this time of latent possibilities and planting seeds for new dreams, connect with the power of the new moon to empower your vision for your work. Envision it coming into reality in your journey today; use all your senses to create a full picture of this dream. If you don't know the details yet, that's fine, focus on what it *feels* like.

Journey

Envision your work as you want it to be.

Waxing Moon

ABUNDANCE RITUAL

What does abundance mean to you? What is abundant *enough*? The building energy of the waxing moon is a perfect time for setting intentions around healthy growth. Let's ask for a ritual to welcome what we need and want into our lives—in a quantity that is actually good for us.

Journey

Journey to ask for a ritual of abundance.

Full Moon

FULL MOON MANIFESTATION CEREMONY

The full moon is the perfect time to align with the cycles of the natural world to help infuse your visions with power. Create a simple ceremony to honor one of your visions. Ask for help in aligning with the power of creation, fertility, and manifestation that the full moon embodies.

Journey

Journey for a full moon ceremony of manifestation and perform it today.

FULL MOON CEREMONY

Ask for (and then perform) a ceremony that helps you enter this phase with clarity and balance. Ask to be shown the next steps, and to have the power to take them. Go outside and greet the big, beautiful moon as she shines down on you.

Journey

Please show me a ceremony to reveal my next steps and empower me to take them.

Waning Moon

RELEASING GRACEFULLY

After fullness comes release. The tide comes in, the tide goes out. After a big exciting day, we need sleep. After any day we need sleep! Have you ever had a big event, like finals week, or a presentation at work, something you had to keep it together for, and when it was over, instead of just relaxing you got the flu or a migraine and crashed? After periods of intensity, we especially want to pay attention to the way we ease into the time of release and slow down. The waning moon can help us learn how to do that gracefully.

Journey

Journey and feel the energy of the waning moon. Sense the gentleness of this cycle of release and wind down. Do any insights come to you about how to apply the wisdom of this cycle to your life?

Solstices and Equinoxes: Ceremonies and Journeys

These four points of the year hold deep practical and symbolic meaning. For thousands of years, we've marked the summer and winter solstices and the spring and fall equinoxes as important junctures in the shifting cycle of the seasons. We note them to help us relate to the physical world—to the balance of light to dark, times of fertility and growth, and times of dissolution and fallowness. And we also celebrate them as a time to look within, to see those same aspects reflected within ourselves.

Indigenous people honored these powerful days by building extraordinary monuments across the globe. In the Incan city of Machu Picchu is a large stone clock called Intihuatana, "the place to which the sun was tied." Its four corners align with the cardinal directions and accurately note the solstices and equinoxes. In Ireland, a small room within the astonishing stone structure of Newgrange is illuminated at dawn for five days every year around the winter solstice. The Great Pyramid of Giza is aligned to the cardinal directions with amazing precision. If you stand near the Sphinx at the summer solstice, the sun appears to set directly between two pyramids. These are just a few examples of the many structures across the globe that honor these powerful times of year.

Although now it may be less urgent to track the movements of the sun for our survival, we are still inextricably linked to the orbiting of the planet. We are part of nature's movements, the ebb and flow and cyclical patterns that all the other aspects of our environment are driven by and attuned to. The more we can intentionally create harmony with those cycles, the better for our health and well-being, and the more we can understand and create good relationships to the world around us.

))●((

Spring Equinox

WHAT IS READY TO SPRING INTO YOUR LIFE?

During the spring, or vernal equinox, we welcome one season and say goodbye to another. The fresh, fertile energy of spring is a dynamic force for change. What is ready to come into your life today in this vibrant season of spring?

Journey

What is ready to come into my life in this season?

REBIRTH AND CELEBRATION

This time of year is about renewal. The word Easter actually comes from an early Saxon goddess of fertility, *Eostre* or *Eastra*, whose name means "spring." Her counterparts from many other cultures were also celebrated at this time of year. Whatever your spiritual beliefs, may you be inspired by the sacredness of this time of renewal and celebration of life. May you receive the blessings and the abundance of the season with joy.

Journey

Celebrate the sacred renewal of this season with a journey to feel the spirit of spring.

SEEDS

In early spring, some fresh green shoots start to break the soil while it's still cold; others stay nestled in the cool dark earth waiting for the real warm-up to begin. They grow at their own pace, according to their own natures, and ultimately bear fruit (or flowers or veggies). In your life, what seeds are you planting? Have you created rich soil for the seed of a new relationship, or for an established one to thrive? Are you planting the seed of a new project or business venture? Are you sowing new ways of thinking, being, or communicating?

Journey

Meditate on what seeds you are sowing, and if they are the right ones for what you want to reap in the future.

Summer Solstice

BE RADIANT

During the time around the summer solstice, the longest day of the year, let's give thanks to our brilliant sun, and shine a little brighter in its honor.

Journey

Journey to the spirit of the Sun. Feel its life-giving warmth surround you. Ask how you can radiate your own light more fully.

ILLUMINATION

At this time of year we spend the balance of our time in the light. Is there any particular aspect of your life that is ready to be fully illuminated as well?

Journey

What is ready to be illuminated in my life today?

EVOLUTION

Summer is potent! So much is alive in the natural world right now, evolving into vibrant stages of being. Let's focus on our own evolution. Is there anything you need, or that should be cleared away, for your evolution to be smooth and unimpeded?

Journey

In the form of decree, create an affirmation of gratitude for your evolution, such as: Thank you for allowing my evolution to be smooth and unimpeded.

Fall Equinox

SEASONAL SHIFT

As the fall equinox approaches, the heat and outward energy of summer winds down and shifts into the cooling inward energy of fall. With the change of each season we have the opportunity to shift ourselves to mirror what's happening in the natural world and to take advantage of the energies that are present, as when cyclists draft on trucks or other cyclists in front of them, but safely! You get the benefit of the forward momentum that is already there, and it pulls you along, too. How can you draft on nature's forward movement as we shift into fall?

Journey

How can I shift most effectively into the next season of fall?

WHAT IS READY TO FALL OUT OF YOUR LIFE?

During the autumnal equinox, we welcome in one season and say goodbye to another. What is ready to fall out of your life during this season, where so much is released and then reabsorbed, creating fuel for new life later in the year?

Journey

What is ready to fall out of my life in this season?

EQUILIBRIUM ON THE EQUINOX

At the time of the fall equinox, day and night are (more or less) evenly balanced. A state of balance rarely lasts long. More often in personal and larger cycles, we fall out of balance, return to it, and then fall back out again. The degree to which we fall out of balance determines how hard we have to work to find our equilibrium again.

Journey

In what ways can I find, and keep, my equilibrium during this time?

))●((

Winter Solstice

MOVE INTO DARKNESS

Around the winter solstice, darkness prevails. How can you use this time, as nature does, to allow areas of your life to lie fallow as needed? Would you benefit from some hibernation, downtime, or the opportunity to focus inward in deep ways?

Journey

How can I make the best use of the darkness?

Hibernation

Hibernating bears go through remarkable physiological changes. Despite the period of inactivity, they metabolize body fat and retain muscle mass, and their cholesterol levels shoot up (twice as high as the cholesterol levels of most humans), yet they don't experience any of the negative effects that we do, like arteriosclerosis or gallstones.

Have you ever wondered what it would be like to hibernate? To sleep so deeply that your body's systems change how they work and everything slows down profoundly? I'm fascinated by how our physical and spiritual lives would change if we did some form of hibernating, perhaps only symbolically. Imagine the dreaming! Most of our lives are not structured to allow for extended periods of stillness, but how about a hibernating day?

Journey

- If possible, hibernate a little today in ordinary reality: rest, sleep, dream.

- Perhaps journey to a bear spirit and ask what it's like and what you can learn that would be useful in your life right now.

- Journey and ask to have a hibernating experience. When we journey we are outside of linear time, so a "short" journey may feel like a long cozy winter in the den!

LIGHT FROM DARKNESS

Although this time of year involves physical darkness, it is often associated with divine light. As we turn inward, perhaps with less distraction from the outside world, how might we use this time to explore the spark of the divine that exists always?

Journey

During this time of outer darkness, feel yourself surrounded by the light of the divine in any form you feel comfortable with.

FAQ

What if nothing happens?

Don't worry. Take a break, review the steps and your intention. Take your time relaxing and shifting out of your ordinary state of mind. It's okay to have a balance between active and passive, between things seeming to "happen" without much or any input from you and taking a more active role in intentionally moving yourself around in the spiritual realms, or experimenting with what happens if you use your imagination at times. Be patient.

What if I don't meet a helping spirit?

Take your time and explore, there is much to learn from the environment. Make sure your intention for the journey is clear before you start. Don't give up. Show your willingness to return.

What if I don't like drumming?

Drumming is the most common way to journey, but it is not the only way. Experiment with other sounds, like music, rattling, didgeridoo, or silence and see what works best for you. Also, the drumming may simply take a little getting used to.

What if I am making it all up?

What if you are? If you receive accurate and valuable information, it might not matter ultimately. However, for the sake of your journeying experiences, if you must debate about their real or imaginary nature, do it after the journeys themselves. Having discernment is healthy, but if you are engaging in the dialogue during the experience, it's very hard to sink into it. Michael Harner suggested simply telling yourself that you are making it *all* up, so that you can preempt the conversation entirely, defusing its power to distract you. After you've been journeying a while, this will likely become less of an issue.

What if I meet something that scares me?

Generally, the spiritual realms of Upper and Lower worlds provide experiences that are for our benefit, even if they are occasionally uncomfortable, disconcerting, or even scary. Working through those emotions may be part of your experience, learning, and healing. However, you should exercise sensible boundaries for, control over, and discernment regarding what is right for you while journeying. Say, "Yes, please," or "No thank you." Simply return from a journey (retracing your steps if possible) if it is really too upsetting or frightening for you at the time.

Do I need to have faith or belief in shamanism to journey?

Shamanism is based on experience, not faith. Have your own experience and then decide what you believe. Bring an open mind about what is possible. We tend to filter out what we can't imagine, and that could limit your experiences.

For more personalized journey advice, it's helpful to have a human teacher. Please see the Resources section for finding one who is ethical and well trained.

Notes

10 access to sacred land:
Jack F. Trope, "Existing Federal Law and the Protection of Sacred Sites: Possibilities and Limitations," *Cultural Survival Quarterly,* December 1995, www.culturalsurvival. org/publications/cultural-survival-quarterly/existing-federal-law-and-protection-sacred-sites; "Rules Governing the Court of Indian Offenses," March 30, 1883, www.nlm. nih.gov/nativevoices/timeline/364. html; en.wikisource.org/ wiki/Code_of_Indian_Offenses.

Evenki people of Siberia:
Mircea Eliade, *Shamanism: Archaic Techniques of Ecstasy* (Princeton: Princeton University Press, 1964), 4; Berthold Laufer, "Origin of the Word Shaman," *American Anthropologist,* 19, no. 3 (July–September 1917): 361–62. doi.org/10.1525/aa.1917.19.3.02a00020.

(Inuit of the Arctic regions):
Eliade, *Shamanism*, 58.

***mudang* (Korea):**
Chongho Kim, *Korean Shamanism: The Cultural Paradox* (Oxon: Routledge, 2018), 32.

***znakharka* (Ukraine):**
Katheryn M. Linduff and Karen S. Rubinson (eds.), *Are All Warriors Male?: Gender Roles on the Ancient Eurasian Steppe* (Plymouth, UK: AltaMira Press, 2008), 71.

***p'aqo* (Andean/Quecha):**
Anna Przytomska-La Civita, "*Apus*: Non-human persons in the ontology of the Q-eros from the Cordillera Vilcanota (Peru)," *Etnografía*, (December 2019): 35–63. doi.org/10.26881/etno.2019.5.03.

***kami* (Mongolia):**
Eliade, *Shamanism*, 4.

***sukya* (Miskito and Sumu):**
Eduard Conzemius, *Ethnographical Survey of the Miskito and Sumu Indians of Honduras and Nicaragua*, Smithsonian Institutions Bureau of American Ethnology, United States Government, Bulletin 106. University of Michigan Library (January 1932): 172.

***sangoma* (South Africa):**
Robert Thorton, "The Transmission of Knowledge in South African Traditional Healing" *Africa* 79, no.1 (February 2009): 17–34. DOI:10.3366/E0001972008000582.

***taltós* (Hungary):**
Eliade, *Shamanism*, 126.

***dukun* (Indonesia):**
Graham Harvey and Robert J. Wallis, *Historical Dictionary of Shamanism*, 2nd ed. (Lanham: Rowman & Littlefield, 2016), 143.

***wu* (China):**
Eliade, *Shamanism*, 454.

11 at least 40,000 years:
Sandra Ingerman, "Shamanism: Healing of Individuals and the Planet" (nd), www.sandraingerman.com/abstractonshamanism.html.

19 **"the energy of nature":**
Leonardo Boff, *Come, Holy Spirit: Inner Fire, Giver of Life, and the Comforter of the Poor* (Maryknoll: Orbis Books, 2015) np.

"to liberate their spirits":
Gershon Winkler, *Travels with the Evil Inclination: Rabble-Rousing Renegade Rabbi's Story* (Berkeley: North Atlantic Books, 2004) 208.

20 **"sonic driving":**
Harner, Michael, *Cave and Cosmos: Shamanic Encounters with Another Reality* (Berkeley: North Atlantic Books, 2013), 44.

"using a drum":
Michael Harner, The Foundation for Shamanic Studies, shamanism.org/workshops/index.php.

45 **"one who sees":**
Michael Harner, *Cave and Cosmos*, 49.

"seeing with the heart":
Ibid., 50.

66 **depression, and PTSD:**
Emma Seppälä, "18 Science-Backed Reasons to Try Loving-Kindness Meditation: Loving-Kindness Meditation packs a punch when it comes to health and happiness," *Psychology Today*, September 15, 2014, www.psychologytoday.com/us/blog/feeling-it/201409/18-science-backed-reasons-try-loving-kindness-meditation.

75 **"by nearly 60 percent":**
"People who give, live longer: U-M study shows," *Michigan News—University of Michigan*, November 12, 2002, news.umich.edu/people-who-give-live-longer u m study shows.

82 **"astral light":** Barbara Brennan, *Hands of Light: A Guide to Healing Through the Human Energy Field* (New York: Bantam Books, 1987), 29.

"as above so below":
Gary Lachman, *The Quest for Hermes Trismegistus: From Ancient Egypt to the Modern World* (Edinburgh: Floris Books 2011), np.

92 **fungus of Oregon:**
Jason Daley, "This Humongous Fungus Is as Massive as Three Blue Whales," *Smithsonian Magazine*, 2018, www.smithsonianmag.com/smart-news/mushroom-massive-three-blue-whales-180970549.

for robust health:
Paul Stamets, *Mycelium Running: How Mushrooms Can Help Save the World* (New York: Ten Speed Press, 2005), 28.

98 **distinguishing friend from foe:**
Michelle Nijhuis, "Friend or Foe? Crows Never Forget a Face, It Seems," *New York Times*, Aug. 25, 2008, www.nytimes.com/2008/08/26/science/26crow.html.

117 **noise pollution:**
Carolyn Gregoire, "Why Silence Is So Good For Your Brain," *Huffington Post*, January 9, 2017, www.huffingtonpost.com/entry/silence-brain-benefits_us_56d83967e4b0000de4037004; Amy Novotney, "Silence please: Psychologists are increasing awareness of the harmful effects noise has on cognition and health," *American Psychological Association*, 42, no.7 (July/August 2011) Print version: page 46, www.apa.org/monitor/2011/07-08/silence.

136 self-expression, and well-being:
Sanne Theodora et al., "Promoting positive outcomes
through strengths interventions: A literature review," *The
Journal of Positive Psychology*, 13:6 (2018): 573–85, DOI:10.
1080/17439760.2017.1365164.

142 combined with repatterning of behavior, can:
Bernard J. Luskin, "The Habit Replacement Loop:
Managing habit formation can lead to greater long-term
student success," *Psychology Today* (May 14, 2017), www.
psychologytoday.com/us/blog/the-media-psychology-
effect/201705/the-habit-replacement-loop; David T. Neal
et al., "Habits—A Repeat Performance," *SAGE Journals*
(August 2006), doi.org/10.1111/j.1467-8721.2006.00435.x.

187 "breathe or blow into":
"Breathing Life Into 'Inspire:' The word's origins are
quite literal," www.merriam-webster.com/words-at-play/
the-origins-of-inspire.

191 by jail or worse:
Dennis Zotigh, "Native Perspective on the 40th
Anniversary for the American Indian Religious Freedom
Act," *Smithsonian National Museum of the American
Indian,* November 30, 2018, www.smithsonianmag.com/
blogs/national-museum-american-indian/2018/11/30/
native-perspectives-american-indian-religious-freedom-act.

204 enhancing immune function:
Juyoung Lee, et al., "Effect of Forest Bathing on
Physiological and Psychological Responses in Young
Japanese Male Subjects," *Public Health* 125, no.2 (February
2011): 93–100. www.sciencedirect.com/science/article/
abs/pii/S0033350610003203?via%3Dihub; Bum Jin Park,
et al., "The Physiological Effects of Shinrin-Yoku (Taking
in the Forest Atmosphere or Forest Bathing): Evidence
from Field Experiments in 24 Forests Across Japan,"

Environmental Health and Preventative Medicine 15, no.1 (Jan 2010):18–26. www.ncbi.nlm.nih.gov/pmc/articles/ PMC2793346/; Marc G. Berman et al., "The Cognitive Benefits of Interacting With Nature," *Psychological Science* 19, no.12 (December 2008): 1207–12. journals.sagepub. com/doi/10.1111/j.1467-9280.2008.02225.x.

241 "a way of caring for each other":
Robin Kimmerer, *Gathering Moss: A Natural and Cultural History of Mosses.* (Corvallis: Oregon State University Press, 2003), 100.

319 sometimes through telepathy:
Jason Cressey, "Making a Splash in the Pacific: Dolphin and Whale Myths and Legends of Oceania," *Rapa Nui Journal: Journal of the Easter Island Foundation* 12, no. 3 (September 1998): 75. kahualike.manoa.hawaii.edu/cgi/ viewcontent.cgi?article=1276&context=rnj.

415 if you focus softly around the edges:
"Averted Vision," *Oxford Reference* (nd) www. oxfordreference.com/view/10.1093/oi/ authority.20110803095437893.

417 pulse rates, and cortisol levels:
Margaret M. Hansen et al., "Shinrin-Yoku (Forest Bathing) and Nature Therapy: A State-of-the-Art Review," *International Journal of Environmental Research and Public Health 14*, no. 8, (July 2017): 851. doi:10.3390/ ijerph14080851.

423 experiencing others' trauma too intensely:
Eytan Halevi and Yael Idisis, "Who helps the helper? Differentiation of self as an indicator for resisting vicarious traumatization," *Psychological Trauma: Theory, Research, Practice, and Policy* 10, no.6, (2018): 698–705. psycnet.apa. org/record/2017-45358-001.

424 (very different experiences within the brain):

Anne Hofmeyer et al., "Contesting the term 'compassion fatigue': Integrating findings from social neuroscience and self-care research," *Elsevier* 23 (October 2019), doi. org/10.1016/j.colegn.2019.07.001; Olga Klimecki and Tania Singer, "Empathic distress fatigue rather than compassion fatigue? Integrating findings from empathy research in psychology and social neuroscience," in *Pathological altruism* eds. B. Oakley, A. Knafo, G. Madhavan, & D. S. Wilson (New York: Oxford University Press, 2012), 368–83.

429 "the sun was tied":

Johan G. Reinhard, *Machu Picchu: Exploring an Ancient Sacred Center,* 4th Edition (Los Angeles: UCLA, The Cotsen Institute of Archeology Press, 2007), 63.

around the winter solstice:

Robert Hensey, *First Light: The Origins of New Grange* (Oxford: Oxbow Books, 2015).

between two pyramids:

Giulio Magli, *Architecture, Astronomy and Sacred Landscape in Ancient Egypt* (New York: Cambridge University Press, 2013), 97.

434 arteriosclerosis or gallstones:

Mark J. Biel and Kerry A. Gunther, "Denning and Hibernation Behavior," National Park Service; Yellowstone. (nd), www.nps.gov/yell/learn/nature/denning.htm.

Acknowledgments

With deep appreciation for the following:
my editor at Kensington Publishing, Denise Silvestro
my agent at Ayesha Pande Literary, Stephany Evans
my book midwife, Caroline Pincus
my many teachers, in many forms
my ancestors in body and spirit
Mother Earth, and our family of
animals, plants, and elements
my friends, especially Wendy
my family, especially my parents
my partner and love, John
my daughter and absolute joy, Violet
Without some of you, this book wouldn't be what it is;
without others, I wouldn't be who I am.
Many of you fall in both categories.

I'm forever grateful.

Resources

For more information about Mara, including links
to additional books, articles, meditation and journey
resources, classes, and the event calendar, please visit:

WholeSpirit.com

ALSO BY MARA

365 Journeys: Shamanism for Every Day
Daily journey delivery and journal

Inner Divinity: Crafting Your Life with Sacred Intelligence
Available in paperback and eBook
from your bookseller of choice

Inner Divinity Crafting Your Life with Sacred Intelligence
Companion series of guided meditations
Available on iTunes